"Overall, this is a book that repays careful reading. It is wise."
Mark Uncles, Heinz Professor of Brand Management, Bradford Management Centre

"... very thought-provoking and readable ... strongly recommend brand managers and design managers involved in packaging design in any market to read it."
Marketing Magazine

"... a radical manifesto for packaging design, eschewing the superficial label decoration created by the 'Twinkies' and the shelf-shout obsession of the 'Logo-louts' in favour of seeing brand identity in terms of the whole pack ... A must-read for any designer."
Graphics International

"The book is written in a personal and easily understood style, appropriate for a wider readership."
Packaging Week

"In a clear and economic style, with many anecdotal examples from the marketing industry, Paul Southgate explains the theory behind Total Branding ... essential reading for marketing professionals and students of marketing and design management."
Package Print & Design

ABOUT THE AUTHOR

Paul Southgate is chief executive of Wickens Tutt Southgate, one of Europe's leading specialists in brand strategy and design.

This book grows directly out of his experience advising some of the world's top marketing companies such as Esso, Coca-Cola, Mars and Unilever.

He started his career on the client side, in brand management with Procter and Gamble, working for four years on such brands as Head & Shoulders, Flash and Bold.

In 1984 he moved into advertising and learned the value of strategic planning at Abbott Mead Vickers, before he pioneered the use of planning techniques in design at Michael Peters (he was the design industry's first ever planning director). He has presented papers on the role of planning in design at the MRS and many industry conferences and is currently a director of the Design Business Association.

TOTAL BRANDING BY DESIGN

How to Make Your Brand's Packaging More Effective

PAUL SOUTHGATE

KOGAN
PAGE

First published in 1994
Paperback edition published in 1995

Kogan Page Limited
120 Pentonville Road
London N1 9JN

© Paul Southgate, 1994

British Library Cataloguing in Publication Data

A CIP record for this book is available from the British Library.

ISBN 0 7494 1864 8

Typeset by Saxon Graphics Ltd, Derby
Printed and bound in Great Britain by Biddles Ltd, Guildford and
Kings Lynn

Jacket illustrations by Adam Young

CONTENTS

CONTENTS

LIST OF PLATES

PREFACE

This book is written for marketing people, and in particular for those marketing people working with packaged goods. It is about a marketing tool whose importance is increasingly coming to be recognized, but which is still undervalued and often ill-used. It is about packaging design, and how best to use it to increase a brand's profitability.

Marketing people spend a great deal of their time, and by far the greatest part of their budgets, on advertising. Advertising is glamorous, it's fun, it's expensive, and quite often it even seems to work. It builds sales.

But this book sets out to show that marketeers, in focusing so intently on advertising, are often missing an enormous trick. It sets out to show that if they spent a corresponding amount of time and energy on their packaging design, they could achieve even better sales results – and at a fraction of the cost.

This is not to belittle the importance of advertising. Every good marketeer these days knows that a brand is no more or less than 'a set of values in the mind of the consumer', and advertising certainly has a significant role to play in creating and sustaining those values.

But, in the words of my creative partner Mark Wickens: 'There are no ads at point-of-sale, where it really matters. Only packs. There are no ads at home in the cupboard to reinforce brand values every time we use a product. Only packs. There are no ads on display in the bathroom or in the drinks cabinet saying who we are (because we are what we buy). Only packs.'

So the pack can have an even more crucial role than

advertising in creating and sustaining brand values, because the pack (unlike the ad) is there at the times when it really matters – at the moment of decision to buy, and at the moment when the product is being experienced in use.

The beauty of it is, the medium itself is free – or rather, it is already built into the costs of production. Packaging is not an optional extra. For the overwhelming majority of brands, it is a functional necessity. Growing environmental awareness is thankfully exerting an increasing influence over the *amount* of packaging used, to cut down on waste, and on the *materials* used, to encourage recycling or re-use. But products need packaging of some sort, so (again unlike advertising) the question is not whether to do it at all. The only question is whether to do it well or badly.

Too often at the moment it is done badly. This book proposes a better way.

ACKNOWLEDGEMENTS

The author wishes to thank:

Elizabeth and Bob Southgate; Mark Wickens, his creative partner and inspiration; all those with whom or for whom he has worked down the years, especially Peter Dee and Leslie Butterfield; David Beard for designing the cover of this book; Nicole Lanitis for her research assistance; all his clients and colleagues at Wickens Tutt Southgate Ltd, without whom this book would have been a little on the thin side; and above all, his wife Natalie for everything, including her good humoured tolerance when the final chapter of this book was still being drafted on the plane en route to Sydney for their wedding.

The author would like to thank the following companies for supplying visual material for this book:

Perrier/Infoplan PR
IDV UK Ltd
CPC (UK) Ltd
Procter & Gamble (US)
Procter & Gamble Ltd
HJ Heinz Company Ltd
Marblehead Trading
SmithKline Beecham plc
SC Johnson
Parfums Cacharel
RHM Foods
Lever Brothers Limited
Ogilvy & Mather

1

INTRODUCTION

THE MEANING OF BRANDING

Branding, according to popular marketing mythology, began with the great ranch-owners and cattlemen in the Wild West. They would literally 'brand' their cattle, communicating a clear message to others, which said 'hands off, this is mine'.

Branding as a marketing tool has nowadays come to have completely the opposite purpose. It says 'hands on, this is for you'.

The underlying concept of branding, however, has not changed as much as this shift in purpose might suggest. From the ranch-owner to the producer of consumer goods, branding has always been – at the most basic level – about asserting ownership.

The difference is that where once the assertion of ownership was a purely defensive ploy – to make it harder for competitors to steal the ranch-owner's products – it is now both defensive and aggressive: defensive in that a strong brand will deter competitors from trying to steal the brand-owner's market, and aggressive in that a strong brand will actively communicate with potential consumers on a multiplicity of levels, giving them all sorts of seductive reasons to buy.

Along the way, the very meaning of the word 'brand' has become much broader and more sophisticated.

To the cattlemen, a 'brand' was simply a mark – no more, no less. To decipher or decode this mark, you needed to know which rancher was in the habit of using that particular mark on his cattle. Even then, the information was of little use unless you knew something about the rancher in question. How strong was he? Where was he based? How many cattle did he own? How many men did he have working for him? The mark itself was of no help in answering these questions. It was simply a mark.

Nowadays, a brand is much more than just a mark. It is, according to marketing guru Peter Doyle, 'a name, symbol, design or some combination which identifies the product of a particular organization as having a sustainable differentiated advantage'.

But even Doyle does not go far enough. I prefer Paul Feldwick's definition of a brand as 'the intangible values created by a badge of reassurance'. Feldwick is the Planning Director of BMP, the advertising agency which – more than any other over the last twenty years or so – has pioneered the use of ever more sophisticated research techniques to develop an understanding of the relationship between consumers and brands.

Note how in Feldwick's words the 'brand' is no longer synonymous with the 'mark' but has become instead a bigger, more abstract, concept. It is a set of 'intangible values', albeit one that is *created* by a 'badge' or mark.

In other words, the mark is not the brand. The mark is merely the *symbol* or *sign* of the brand.

This is an important distinction. To think of a brand not as a name or logo or graphic mark, but rather as a set of 'intangible values', is to start to think about branding in a much more sophisticated and powerful way.

Understanding brands in this way has been one of the most fundamental developments in recent marketing history. It is one of the key factors explaining the difference between today's successful brands, and the less successful.

If you think of a brand only as a mark denoting ownership, you can slap it on anything – and many brand owners still do. But this is to use branding in its crudest and simplest form. It is to use branding in the same way as the Wild West ranchers used it, simply to say 'this is mine'.

To think of a brand as a set of 'intangible values', by contrast, is to understand something which is absolutely crucial in the successful development of brands today. And that is that brands do not exist, in any meaningful sense, in the factory or even in the marketing department. They exist in the consumer's mind.

A QUESTION OF OWNERSHIP

Brands, as the better marketeers have come to realize, do not really belong to the manufacturer. They belong to the consumer.

Of course, if a brand exists in the consumer's mind, then somebody has to have put it there. And in the early stages of a brand's life, it does still belong to the manufacturer (or indeed service-provider – for too long, brands were only thought about in the context of manufactured goods, whereas in truth the principles of branding apply equally well to services).

It is up to the manufacturer or service-provider in these early stages to decide what he or she wants the brand's 'intangible values' to be. The mark itself (Doyle's 'name, symbol design or some combination') is only one of the tools available to help create and communicate those values.

But there comes a point in a brand's life when ownership is subtly transferred to the consumer. Beyond this point, perception is reality. The brand's values are no more and no less than what the consumer *believes* them to be.

The marketing person's job thereafter is to try to manage those perceptions and beliefs as best he or she can – to build on those perceptions which add value to the product or service in question, to try to eliminate those perceptions which don't, to keep the brand's values relevant in the light of changing consumer lifestyles and changing competition, but always to remember that ownership of the brand resides now in the consumer's mind, and that the consumer will resist anything which contradicts his or her beliefs about that brand.

Paradoxically, the consumer's ownership of a brand is both a great help and a great hindrance to the modern marketeer.

It is a help in that, once a particular set of 'intangible values' has become firmly lodged in the consumer's mind, those values are very difficult to undermine (witness the successful come-back of Perrier following that brand's enforced withdrawal due to benzene contamination in 1989).

19

Yet it is a hindrance for the same reason. In the UK, BhS is now a retail brand offering a stylish and modern range of merchandise, but it will be several years before consumers fully 'forget' their beliefs about dowdy old British Home Stores. Toyota built a worldwide reputation for good value cars at the bottom end of the market, and found it could not simply slap the mark (or, in the car world, 'marque') on luxury models, because the brand – in the consumer's mind – did not belong in the luxury sector. The company had to invent a new brand – Lexus – to compete in that sector.

Consumers can be surprisingly stubborn in clinging to their beliefs about some brands. In blind taste-tests, American consumers overwhelmingly preferred the taste of new Coke to the original product. But they *believed* that original Coke was the best-tasting cola and famously resisted the new-tasting product when it was launched as a replacement for the original.

However, consumers can sometimes be only too willing to accept changes in a brand's values – indeed, they can sometimes get there quicker than the brand's owners. Several of our clients have had the experience of researching new product ideas, with a view to launching them as extensions to well-known brand names, only to find that consumers were convinced that the brands in question already included these new products as part of their ranges. In each case, the product in question had such an obviously good 'fit' with their existing perceptions of the brand, and added to the brand's values in such obviously desirable ways, that consumers could not believe it was not on the market already!

The question of how far a brand's values can be made to stretch is discussed in more detail in Chapter 4. For the moment, suffice it to say that a brand can stretch only so far as consumers *believe* it can stretch, because it's their brand, not ours. It is the 'set of values' in their heads.

Most marketeers these days understand this very well, though a surprising number still think of a brand as simply a name, logo or mark.

What is *not* sufficiently understood – even by those for whom the concept of a brand as a 'set of values' is deeply ingrained – is the implication that this has for the main subject of this book: packaging design.

PACKAGING DESIGN AND BRANDING

It is only recently that the giant marketing companies have come to take packaging design seriously as a marketing tool. Even today, most do not really understand its power, or how to use it properly. Most still give it insufficient management attention, delegating responsibility for packaging design to the most junior personnel and giving them inadequate budgets to use in its development.

This is surprising when one thinks of the pivotal contribution packaging design has made to some of the world's most successful and long-established brands.

Think of the famous Coke bottle. It now accounts for a minuscule proportion of sales of Coca-Cola, having long ago succumbed to the cost advantages and production efficiencies of cans. But the bottle was an enormously potent contributor to, and symbol of, the brand values of Coke in its early years, and continues to be used as the 'lead' packaging format in developing markets. When cans were first introduced, they featured a graphic representation of the bottle, and recently Coca-Cola have re-introduced this unusual approach to packaging design (putting a picture of a bottle on a can is rather odd, let's face it, but speaks volumes for the iconic power of the distinctive bottle design). And the bottle is the definitive brand symbol in worldwide advertising campaigns for Coca-Cola.

If you think of Jack Daniels, you immediately think of the distinctive square bottle and the black label with its ornate 'crafted' typography. The brand and the pack are inseparable in the mind's eye (see Plate 3).

Bovril has always been a byword for beefiness, in part because of its beefy-looking jar (see Plate 4). The Perrier bottle exudes French elegance (see Plate 1). In the US, the Tide pack, with its colourful and dynamic graphics, for years communicated the ultimate in cleaning power (see Plate 5). More recently, in Europe, the Ariel 'atomium' became a potent symbol for advanced 'biological' action (see Plate 6).

Yet many of these examples, especially the early ones, happened more by accident than design. Legend has it that the design for the Coca-Cola script (see Plate 2) was created by the company's accountant! For the most part, packaging design has historically been a very hit-or-miss affair. An obvious exception has been in the field of perfumes, where the importance of packaging has always been recognized. Indeed, many perfume houses will admit off the record that the packaging is more critical than the fragrance itself in determining a brand's success or failure.

But in the mainstream of consumer goods marketing, few companies until recently used packaging design as it should be used. The conscious and deliberate use of packaging design to encapsulate and communicate brand values was the exception rather than the rule.

In some companies, packaging was not even considered to be the province of the marketing department. Because packaging has to work first and foremost on the functional levels (product protection, filling efficiency, distribution and handling efficiency, etc) it was often left to the production department. So far as marketing was concerned, it was enough that the pack carried the brand's logo.

The climate of opinion really started to change with the publication in 1961 of James Pilditch's book *The Silent Salesman*. Packaging was now being recognized as a marketing tool – or at least as a sales tool: 'The package as salesman – that is the new role. It is the connecting link between company and customer – the sales clincher. After all your research, promotion and distribution, the product arrives on a shelf. The final step, from shelf to shopping basket, depends on the package.'

This all seems rather obvious now, but in 1961 to many marketeers this was a new thought. Pilditch pointed out that this new role was 'the inescapable consequence of a marketing system that depends more and more on self-service'. And it is true that in the days when personal service was the norm in shopping – even for grocery products – packaging design did not need to work quite so hard as it does today. But, as Pilditch said, 'thanks to the supermarket and its like, the burden of selling and waiting on customers has fallen increasingly on the package itself'.

Pilditch went on to talk about how packaging design could best adapt to this new role: 'A package must literally shout attention to the product in-store. Yet, after attracting the customer, it must fade into the background and permit the

22

product to come forward.' And, developing Vance Packard's prescription for advertising ('sell the sizzle rather than the meat'), Pilditch pointed out that packaging design has to deal equally well with both sizzle and meat: 'Spark the dream, but sell the reality.'

In defining this new role for packaging, Pilditch concentrated mainly on its potential for clinching the one-off sale – its contribution to impulse purchase. He had less to say about packaging's broader contribution to the creation and sustenance of long-term brand values.

Nevertheless, he was starting to hint at this broader role when he recognized that the 'silent salesman' did not have to rely exclusively on hard-sell techniques. 'It could be that the time for bold and blatant packaging is past,' he wrote. 'People like sentimentality and need romance.'

He recognized the need for the soft-sell, for emotional, as well as rational, values in packaging design, quoting with approval the dictum of advertising guru David Ogilvy that 'the greater the similarity between products, the less part reason plays in brand selection'.

And he recognized that excellence in packaging design could sometimes add value in its own right: 'the extra benefits given to a product by skilfully designing the package are *enjoyed by the buyer*' (his italics).

But in the end, *The Silent Salesman* was (as its title implied) a book about the pack purely as sales-clincher. Indeed Pilditch defined the packaging designer's job in exactly these terms: 'Put simply, his job is to make things sell.'

Thirty years later, Mary Lewis (Creative Director of the London-based consultancy Lewis Moberly) would write that 'good brand packaging is far more than a salesman. It is also a flag of recognition and a symbol of values.' Echoing Feldwick's words about 'intangible values', Lewis locates the brand firmly in the mind of the consumer, defining a brand as 'the aura of beliefs and expectations about the product which make it relevant and distinctive', and talking about the pack's key role as 'the physical embodiment of a brand's core values ... the pack evokes the essence of what the brand is all about. It is the brand's identity.'

For Lewis, too, packaging has a sales role to play: 'It has the power to engage the consumer in dialogue at the very moment the purchase decision is made. It can work for the brand or against it. It can make or break a sale.' But pack design is no longer purely about shelf-impact, seduction and triggering the impulse-purchase: 'Pack designers are in the process of building *relationships* ... between the brand and consumers.'

So the pack, beyond its purely functional tasks, is also a 'salesman'; and beyond this, it is a builder of long-term relationships in its role as the embodiment of brand values.

If it has to do all this, you would think that packaging design would be taken pretty seriously by marketeers. And increasingly it is. But, in most consumer goods companies, there's still a long way to go.

The UK is generally acknowledged as leading the world in the use of packaging design as a marketing tool. (Japan leads the world in terms of aesthetics, and packaging-as-art-form, but that's another story.)

Part of the reason for the UK's current pre-eminence in this area is as a spin-off from its acknowledged recent pre-eminence in advertising – the two disciplines have much in common, as we shall come on to discuss in Chapters 3 and 4.

But part of the reason is to be found in the phenomenal recent growth, in the UK, of Retail Own Brands.

FROM OWN LABEL TO OWN BRAND

In most of the world, grocery retailers sell manufacturers' branded goods. If they sell anything under their 'Own Label', it tends to be goods of lower quality, sold at a lower price, and packaged in the most basic manner possible. Until the 1980s, that was the case in the UK also. What happened in the 1980s was that UK grocery retailers discovered the power of packaging design. At first using it primarily to mimic the leading manufacturer brands, they soon went beyond this, and started to use packaging design actively to add value in its own right. They discovered that good packaging design, allied to improvements in product quality, could enable them to compete with the manufacturer brands on their own terms. They discovered that with good packaging design, they would not need to undercut the manufacturer brands in price by so much (indeed, in some cases they would not need to undercut at all). And they discovered that they could secure higher margins on Own Labels than on equivalent manufacturer brands.

The result of these discoveries has been that in the UK, in just about every grocery market of any consequence, Own Labels' share has increased dramatically over the last decade, putting the fear of God into the manufacturers of all but the strongest brands.

It was when manufacturers began to realize that better packaging design was one of the key factors behind Own Labels' success that they started to pay more attention to packaging design themselves.

But the story is far from over. American and European retailers have rushed to copy the Own Label success of British retailers like Tesco and Sainsbury. American and European manufacturers are having to think harder about their packaging designs as a result. And meanwhile, in the UK, the game is moving into its next stage.

At the time of writing, UK retailers are *still* using packaging design at only half-power. They have been using it very effectively in the 'silent salesman'. role, seducing the customer into the impulse-purchase of Own Label products. The 'basic' approach has been temporarily resurrected (Tesco's Value range). And recently, some (notably Sainsbury's in attacking Coca-Cola) have reverted to the old tactic of mimicry in order to take on the most strongly entrenched brand leaders – much to the fury of the British Producers and Brand Owners Group, formed to lobby for a strengthening of trade mark protection laws. But, with only a handful of exceptions, retailers have not yet used packaging as effectively as they might in building their own brand values.

Let us be clear about this: in every meaningful sense of the word, Tesco is now a brand; so is Sainsbury; so are Safeway, Waitrose, Asda and the rest. And in every other sphere of marketing activity (store design, advertising, PR, environmental policy, etc) they are all busily defining and communicating their own distinctive brand values. But they are only just beginning to use packaging design in this way. Until recently, if you bought an Own Label product from Tesco, then went out and bought the identical product from Sainsbury, Waitrose and Asda, if you covered up the logos you would not be able to tell which product came from which store.

There was no distinctive Tesco-ness about Tesco's packaging designs, no distinctive Sainsbury-ness about Sainsbury's. They were all good, but they all looked the same. They were not using packaging design to communicate brand values, only to achieve impulse-purchase.

Now they are starting to do both. In other sectors, some retailers (usually those which do not sell manufacturer brands, which may or may not be a coincidence) have been doing this for a while: The Body Shop in toiletries, Marks & Spencer (St Michael) in food, River Island in fashion. These are all true Retail Brands, and they use packaging design as 'the embodiment of their brand values'.

Strangely, there are other markets in which – in terms of their use of packaging design – retailers have yet to get off the starting blocks – in DIY, for example, or electrical goods. But manufacturers in these sectors must know that it is only a matter of time before these retailers, too, get their acts together.

Back in the grocery sector, manufacturers have already had to learn to cope with the emergence of strong Retail Brands. They have learned to pay more attention to packaging design. But if they are going to compete effectively in the future, many of them will have to learn to get better at it.

Which is where 'Total Branding' comes in.

SUMMARY

1. A 'brand' is not a name, logo or graphic device. It is a set of 'intangible values' in the minds of consumers. A strong brand is therefore alive, rich, complex and enormously powerful.

2. Packaging design, once thought of in purely functional terms, then more recently understood as a sales tool, is more helpfully – and more powerfully – perceived as the physical embodiment of brand values.

3. The UK currently leads the world in this field, partly thanks to the discovery of packaging design's value by the major multiple retailers, who are now using it to turn Own Labels into Retail Brands.

4. What has been happening in the UK is already starting to happen in the rest of the world.

5. If manufacturers are to have any future as brand owners, not merely as suppliers to Retail Brands, they will have to become more skilled than most currently are in the use of packaging design as a marketing tool.

2

TOTAL BRANDING

THE BASIC THEORY

Mark Wickens and I coined the phrase 'Total Branding' in 1990 as a shorthand description of the new approach to packaging design which our company, Wickens Tutt Southgate, was struggling towards.

The basic theory of Total Branding is deceptively simple. It is about using the *whole pack* deliberately and actively to communicate brand values. It is about going beyond a memorable logo and trying to use every aspect of a brand's packaging to give it a memorable identity. It is about engaging the consumer's sense of touch (via shape, structure and materials) as well as the sense of sight. It is about using design to communicate brand benefits and personality, not just product features. It is, in short, about making pack design a harder-working contributor to brand values on every level.

All of which may seem obvious enough, and obviously desirable from a marketeer's point of view.

In practice, however, achieving Total Branding requires a fundamentally different approach to managing design projects from that which is in common use today. It requires different thinking (from client and designer alike), different working practices, different research methodologies – and above all, it requires the breaking down of preconceptions about what a brand's packaging *ought* to look like. It takes a brave marketeer to do it, but the rewards are considerable.

The rest of this chapter discusses the theory in more detail.

The rest of this book is about how it works and how to do it.

ACTIVE VERSUS PASSIVE DESIGN

We have already defined packaging design as, among other things, a symbol of a brand's values. These values can be derived from a plethora of sources: where the brand is sold; how it is displayed; who is seen using it; how it is used; who makes it (and what you already know about them); and of course its advertising.

Over time, a brand's packaging design will take on those extrinsically generated values, eventually becoming quite literally *symbolic* of those values.

In this sense, all packaging design operates – more or less successfully, and with time and experience as the key determining variables – on a semiotic level.

Umberto Eco, in his *Theory of Semiotics*, observed that 'a house is an icon of the cultural form or complex combination of forms of which it is a material expression' and that 'every object ... has stimulus value for members of a society only insofar as it is an iconic sign signifying some corresponding form of their culture'.

Packaging design works on exactly this level. In the late 1980s, a bottle of Sol with a sliver of lime in its neck became an iconic sign signifying trendy London media-types (or rather, people who wished to be *seen* as trendy London media-types) trying to look cool in bars. A pack of Persil is an iconic sign signifying ever-caring, ever-smiling motherhood (or at least it did until Lever Bros gave a more dangerously masculine edge to the brand's personality with the introduction of Persil Power. The withdrawal of that product, after allegations that its key ingredient damaged clothes, cost Lever's £57 million and has been seen as a major disaster. In my view, however, the scrapping of Persil Power will be seen in the longer term to have saved the Persil brand; there are many things a brand can do in its lifetime, but changing sex isn't one of them!). The famous Coca-Cola bottle is an iconic sign signifying youthful American exuberance.

All packaging design can work like this. All it takes is time and consumer experience, and the pack will absorb meanings, like a sponge absorbing water.

But this is merely to describe packaging design in its most *passive* mode. On this level, *any* pack design would do the job just as well, because a pack can absorb meanings even if those meanings are far removed from anything inherent in the design of the pack itself.

The Heineken label has become an iconic sign signifying refreshment – yet there is nothing inherently refreshing about the graphics themselves (see Plate 7). Over the years, the Heinz baked beans can has absorbed meanings such as warmth, nutrition, motherhood and nurturing (meanings derived from childhood experience and from advertising) without so much as a hint of those values in the design itself (see Plate 8).

So does this mean packaging design is not so important after all? Well, yes and no. It depends how hard you want your marketing budget to work.

It is true to say that the pack does not *have* to be an active contributor to a brand's values. Any old pack will do if you simply want to sit back and wait for it to absorb meanings and values from other sources – which, eventually, it will.

But what a wasted opportunity! Why not make the pack work harder for you? Why not use it actively to communicate the very values which you wish it (and which the consumer will allow it) to symbolize?

The Perrier bottle is an iconic sign signifying French elegance, and arguably would have become so (thanks in part to its 'eau so expensive' advertising) even if it looked like a bottle of HP sauce. But its ability to symbolize French elegance is surely enhanced by the fact that it looks and feels elegant and French.

The Absolut Vodka bottle is symbolic of brand values such as clean, pure and modern (see Plate 9). How much more time would it have taken (and how much harder would the rest of the brand's marketing mix have had to work) for it to acquire those values if the bottle did not *look* so clean, pure and modern?

All packaging design will, over time, become symbolic of a brand's values. But it will do so quicker and more effectively if it is used actively to communicate those values, not merely to be a passive receptacle for them.

This is vitally important for new brands especially, because these days time is one thing they are seldom given.

NEW BRANDS, AND REPOSITIONING OLD BRANDS

There are a few companies (IDV, for one) which are prepared to take the long-term view, launching new brands and giving them time to establish themselves. But most companies – if only because their retailers demand it – expect virtually instant success, or the new brand is withdrawn.

In these circumstances, using packaging design to its maximum active potential becomes a matter of common sense. And it is interesting to note that even IDV, who will give a new brand several years before passing judgement on it, always try to make their packaging designs as actively communicative as possible: the Baileys bottle doesn't look and feel warm, traditional and Irish by accident (see Plate 10); Malibu, too, has its brand values neatly – and actively – encapsulated in the look of its bottle.

The need to use packaging as actively as possible is equally apparent – if not more so – in repositioning an old brand as it is in launching a new one. As Mary Lewis has said: 'In the delicate business of repositioning brands, the packaging is frequently more important than the advertising, because it forcefully defines the new frame through which you want the consumer to see the brand. In this context, active packaging gives the marketing process broader options.'

Thus, when Allied Breweries wanted to reposition Skol 1080 (which, prior to their merger with Carlsberg, was Allied's only contender in the super-strong lager sector) to upgrade consumer recognition of its quality, it was given a totally new graphic identity based on the visual language of hallmarking (as used by goldsmiths and silversmiths) to communicate as actively as possible the values of craftsmanship with which Allied wished it to be imbued. Consumer response to the new positioning was immediate. Despite negligible advertising support, sales doubled virtually overnight.

Sadly, following the merger, the new-look Skol 1080 was felt to be encroaching on the territory of its now sister-brand Carlsberg Special Brew, so it was repositioned (and therefore redesigned) all over again. Thus is marketing ever the servant of higher corporate goals.

Or consider the role of packaging in the repositioning of SmithKline Beecham's Lucozade brand – one of the most successful repositioning exercises in recent history (see Plate 11). For many years the brand had been positioned as a caring aid to recovery from sickness. Although this was a highly distinctive positioning, it restricted the brand to a small, and not very profitable, niche in the market. Beecham

34

realized – and had the courage to act on the realization – that the core values at the heart of this positioning were to do with 'energizing', and that those values could be re-interpreted to give the brand much broader consumer relevance and appeal. In fact, this may be seen as another example of the consumer having got there first or, at least, having accelerated the repositioning by adopting it in an unforeseen way. Beecham's realization of the full scale of the opportunity was prompted by the observation that Lucozade had been 'discovered' by teenagers in the emerging 'rave' scene in the mid-1980s, and was being drunk instead of alcohol to sustain dance-energy at all-night warehouse parties.

Beecham was quick to capitalize on the opportunity. In place of the historical 'sick-child-in-bed' advertising we now saw garish posters promoting Lucozade as the source of 'N-R-G'. Packaging, though, was the key element in the repositioning. The core brand had been given a more dynamic graphic identity, and smaller single-serve bottles introduced (initially without any tamper-evidence – an oversight which Beecham would regret a few years later, but that's another story). Distribution, now via Britvic, was extended to newsagents and petrol station forecourts as Lucozade started to compete with the famous distribution strategy of Coca-Cola of getting the brand 'within an arm's reach of desire'. Perhaps the most important feature of the repositioning was the decision to speed it up by introducing a new sub-brand, Lucozade Sport, pre-empting the UK launch of 'isotonic' soft drinks such as Gatorade. Lucozade Sport is a pretty good example of Total Branding. The pack formats, standard 330 ml cans and in particular the innovative single-serve foil pouch with integral 'straw', put the brand straightaway in the right usage context. And dynamic graphics and colours are actively used to encapsulate and communicate the brand's core 'energizing' values. The whole pack is the identity, not just the logo.

BRANDING BEYOND THE LOGO

It might be helpful at this point to emphasize the distinction between the *brand* and the *product*.

The distinction should be obvious enough by now. If a brand is a 'set of values' in the mind of the consumer, we have already seen how those values can be derived from factors such as who uses it, where it is sold, what cultural meaning it has – factors which go way beyond the physical features of the product itself. But – perhaps because the brand's values are usually supported by, or stem from, physical *product* features – the distinction can sometimes be blurred, even in the minds of experienced marketeers. Indeed, where the distinction becomes *too* blurred, or when brand values and product features become one and the same, it could be argued that you haven't really got a brand at all. In the UK, Hoover is often cited as an example of this phenomenon. For years, the values of Hoover as a brand were so inextricably bound up in the features of a particular product – the vacuum cleaner – and Hoover's management failed so signally to communicate any added values *beyond* those which derived directly from the product, that Hoover simply became a generic descriptive word for 'vacuum cleaner' – any vacuum cleaner, from any manufacturer. It took two decades of marketing effort, and a good deal of line-extension into other electrical appliance markets, to rescue Hoover from this fate and give it any real meaning as a brand. (More recently, it took only two months, and a supremely cynical sales promotion involving a free-air-tickets offer that was quite literally 'too good to be true', to undo much of the good work, but that again is another story.)

The Hoover lesson is one that is sometimes lost, on food manufacturers in particular. In food markets, the product itself (ingredients, recipe, appetite appeal) is so central to the purchase decision that food packaging often concentrates on straightforward and appetising presentation of the product whilst ignoring all other considerations. The bigger opportunity, to use packaging design to communicate brand values which transcend the features of any one particular product, is often missed.

Design features will be built in to aid brand *recognition* (usually a logo and a uniform background colour – think of the yellow packs of Birds Eye's Captain's Table fish range, or the white Findus Lean Cuisine packs) but that's about as far as it goes. Packaging design can, and should, work harder than this. The need for it to do so is well illustrated by the Dalepak story.

Dalepak is a smallish Yorkshire-based food manufacturer

36

which, in the early 1990s, pioneered the development of vegetable-based frozen convenience foods. The company enjoyed rapid growth with its vegetable burgers, cauliflower-cheese grills, coated vegetable fingers and the like. They had spotted a growing consumer trend to 'occasional vegetarianism' or at least meat reduction, in the mainstream UK population. The big players thought that 'Green Cuisine', as it has become known, would appeal only to out-and-out vegetarians – a growing market, but one thought still too small to be worth bothering with. So Dalepak, having spotted the broader opportunity, had the field virtually to itself for a while.

Inevitably, it didn't last. Once Dalepak had proved that a sizeable market for these products existed, Birds Eye moved in with their 'Country Club Cuisine' range (since renamed 'Vegetable Cuisine').

At the time of writing, Dalepak is struggling desperately to hold on to the market it created, and is suffering huge share losses to Birds Eye. In a sense, Dalepak have only themselves to blame. By the time Birds Eye launched in 1992, Dalepak had become probably the biggest 'invisible brand' in the UK. Vast numbers of people were buying their products, but awareness of Dalepak as a brand was virtually non-existent.

This was partly due to the absence of any significant advertising support.

But I believe the reason for the brand's relative 'invisibility' had even more to do with poor packaging design. If Dalepak had created a strong and memorable brand identity at point-of-sale – if 'the whole pack' had been used, not just to present the product, but to do so in a way which created and communicated distinctive Dalepak brand values – then the brand would have been a lot less vulnerable to Birds Eye. At least consumers would have known whose vegetable burgers they were buying, and would have been given some emotional values with which they could identify.

As it was, Dalepak's packaging designs were unambitious and bland in the extreme. They presented the products in a reasonably appetising way, but apart from a Dalepak logo stuck on in the top left-hand corner, there was nothing to distinguish the packs from the most basic of Own Label offerings, or from the myriad of even smaller companies' frozen vegetable products.

There was only a logo to tell the consumer that these were not just any old vegetable burgers, but Dalepak's! And only a logo is not enough.

Dalepak's packaging has since been re-designed to try to inject some distinctive values based on the brand's provenance in the Yorkshire Dales. It's a step in the right direction, but I fear may prove to be too little too late.

To return to Lucozade Sport, then. One of the reasons it is a strong and successful identity is precisely because it does not depend entirely on the logo for its branding. The whole pack is distinctive. The whole pack encapsulates relevant brand values (energizing, dynamic, youthful). The whole pack is the brand identity. And that's how packaging design *should* be used.

THE ROLE OF SHAPE AND STRUCTURE

Much of what we've been discussing so far has been to do with graphics. And certainly the active use of graphics can go a long way towards achieving Total Branding. But you may have noticed that many of the examples of good packaging already mentioned have involved innovative pack shapes and structures as well as graphics.

Lucozade Sport sells mainly in standard 330 ml cans. But the innovative single-serve foil pouch was hugely important in positioning the brand in the right way. The famous Coca-Cola bottle is famous because it's a unique shape. As is the Perrier bottle. Or the Bovril jar.

Total Branding really comes into its own when it's not just a question of making the whole pack work harder graphically, but structurally as well.

Toilet Duck created – and branded – a whole new category of toilet-cleaners via the structural innovation of a neck shape which directs the product under the toilet rim (see Plate 12). The clever thing about Toilet Duck is the way in which this innovation was not simply launched as a 'new improved bottle' but was used as the focus of a totally integrated brand concept.

Jif lemon juice became the dominant brand in its market by the simple expedient of creating a pack shaped exactly like a lemon!

More recently, my own company has helped consolidate Nestlé's hold on the honey market by designing for its Gales brand a glass jar in the shape of a beehive – what quicker way to communicate the values of purity and naturalness for a honey brand? (see Plate 13) Many manufacturers shy away from even thinking about such structural packaging innovation – either because of the capital expenditure which might be involved in retooling or even rebuilding the filling lines, or else (unforgivably) because structural packaging is felt to be the province of the production department and internal politics stand in the way of progress.

Structural innovation is certainly difficult, and can be expensive, but then the rewards for getting it right can be commensurately higher. There are very few situations in which it is not worth even *considering* the structure as well as graphics.

One such situation – on the face of it – is that of the manufacturer of liquid products (milk, juices, soups, etc) who is locked into Tetrapak. Having invented one of the great physical packaging forms of our age – if, sadly, one of the most infuriatingly difficult to open from the consumer's point of view – the creators of Tetrapak have been extremely astute in retaining control of the technology and 'locking in' their major customers, such that the cost of change can seem prohibitive. But even the Tetrapak people are becoming increasingly open to development and improvement. Environmental concerns are forcing them to experiment with new materials, and they have in recent years (in tandem with their major brand customers and their designers) developed a number of alternative opening and closing mechanisms. Even their oft-derided print capabilities have been slowly improving under pressure from design consultancies.

The breakthrough of a significant improvement in the basic Tetrapak has not yet been achieved. But it will be one day, and it will be the manufacturer who has pushed the hardest who will reap the immediate benefits.

THE SENSE OF TOUCH

Sometimes, relatively minor changes to a brand's physical packaging can make a big difference, for example when

Colgate-Palmolive wanted to relaunch their Soft & Gentle deodorant brand (see Plate 14). Strategically very straightforward (the brand's values are neatly encapsulated in the name itself), giving the brand a totally Soft & Gentle graphic identity was the easy part. The problem was that the brand's values were being undermined by the physical properties of the aerosol can – cold, hard, shiny and metallic. Yet Colgate-Palmolive had several million pounds tied up in existing aerosol technology and could not afford to change.

But even here, by working closely with Colgate's production people, our designers were able (at no significant on-cost) to 'rough-up' the tool for the caps, and to switch to a matt ink finish for the can itself, giving the brand a warmer, more Soft & Gentle feel in the hand – even though the basic aerosol structure itself had not changed.

I mention Soft & Gentle to illustrate an important point – when we talk about structural packaging innovation, we are not only talking about shape, but also about texture. The tactile sensation of a brand in the hand can be just as important as its visual appearance on the shelf.

Indeed, it could be argued that the sense of touch is the last great undiscovered marketing tool – undiscovered because the sense of touch operates almost entirely at the subconscious level.

If you think about it, there are very few occasions during a typical day when you become consciously aware of the sense of touch. Most people can recall with reasonable accuracy an enormous number of things they have *seen* during the course of a normal day, or things they have *heard*. But things they have *touched*? Only at the extremes of experience (sex at one end, perhaps unblocking a sink at the other!) do we become consciously aware of the sense of touch.

But at the subconscious level, we experience the world as a tactile as well as an audio-visual reality. And that includes the brands we buy and use.

If you ask consumers in qualitative research groups to close their eyes, and if you then (in the context of discussing a particular brand or product category) place in their hands an array of different physical materials, it is astonishing the degree to which some will 'feel right' and others feel wholly wrong, each material telling a completely different story about the brand in question. And although consumers do not in reality experience brands with their eyes closed (or not many brands, anyway) it is reasonable to suppose that their feelings about different brands are nevertheless influenced to some degree at least by the tactile sensation of the pack in use.

None of this is to say that we should ignore the more prosaic structural packaging considerations of cost and filling-line efficiency. Only that we should also consider different shapes, materials and textures in terms of what they *communicate* (if only subliminally) about the brand.

PHYSICAL PACKAGING AND BRAND VALUES

A few years ago, Heinz launched their famous tomato ketchup in a squeezable plastic bottle. No doubt they have got reams and reams of market research in support of this move, highlighting the obvious consumer benefits of convenience, reduced weight in the shopping basket, reduced incidence of breakage and so on. But I would be willing to bet that this move will – subtly, and over time – undermine the brand's reputation in consumers' minds as the definitive, thick and rich, tomato ketchup.

Heinz are probably aware of this, and it is doubtless no accident that the brand's advertising has continued to feature the distinctive glass bottle and the need for patience – or a hefty slap administered to the upturned bottle's base – to get the stuff onto the plate.

So why introduce the squeezable plastic bottle at all? The Heinz marketeers have no doubt made a calculated trade-off, hoping that the new pack form would bring sufficient increases in penetration and weight of usage to more than offset any damage it causes to the brand's image.

They may well have been right. It is equally possible, though, that they have underestimated the contribution of physical packaging to a brand's values. Future generations of Heinz tomato ketchup brand managers will have to judge.

There are certain markets, of course, in which the value of physical packaging is very well understood, notably perfumes, cosmetics and drinks. These markets have two important characteristics in common. The first is that the packaging is

41

an integral part of the product experience in use; the level of the consumer's interaction with the pack is high every time he or she uses the product. The second is that differences between the products themselves can in many cases be difficult or even impossible to detect. Few consumers can tell the difference in blind tastings between one lager and another, or one malt whisky and another; one cleansing lotion is much like another; even perfumes, tested 'blind' are different in ways that the consumer finds difficult to pin down.

In these circumstances, it is not surprising that marketeers pay more attention to the physical packaging of such products. The success of Grolsch was built almost entirely on the chunky, heavily embossed glass bottle with its built-in ceramic stopper. Cacherel's Lou Lou has become a successful scent brand partly because it smells nice, but partly too because its distinctively shaped flasks and bottles are felt by young women to look good on their dressing tables and to feel good in use (see Plate 16).

Yet there are other markets which share the key characteristics of lager and cosmetics (high physical interaction, similar product features) which for some reason have not seen such innovation in physical packaging.

Why, for example, are virtually all cigarette packs the same? It's a category which my own company will not get involved in, despite my folly in having been a smoker for many years. But as an interested observer, I find it staggering that the cost-efficiency and DPP* advantages of identikit cigarette packs have prevented any of the major players from trying to get a competitive edge via physical packaging innovation.

Or perhaps they *have* tried, and failed. But it is difficult to believe that a significant market opportunity is not going begging for the want of a little imagination in physical packaging.

In the UK yoghurt market, the German brand Müller was unknown when it was launched in the late 1980s. It became brand leader virtually overnight largely due to a simple

---

*DPP stands for Direct Product Profitability, a calculation increasingly used by retailers to determine the precise profit contribution of each individual line stocked, after taking into account handling costs and the amount of cubic shelf-space it occupies.

physical packaging innovation which allowed it to offer yoghurt and fruit in separate compartments of an otherwise conventional foil-sealed plastic pot, so the consumer can 'mix to taste'. So simple! Yet the success of Müller Fruit Corners seemed to take Ski and the other market leaders by surprise (see Plate 17).

THE DEFINITION TRAP

Often, imagination is curtailed simply by accepted market definitions. What starts as a convenient classification within which to measure market shares ('Brand x has $y\%$ of the canned fruit desserts market') can easily become a conceptual straitjacket from which marketeers seem to find it hard to escape.

Why 'canned fruit desserts'? Consumers don't think like that. They don't think, as they browse along the supermarket aisles, 'Hmm, I think I'll get the kids some canned fruit desserts for their tea tonight!' Yet marketeers often consider their consumers' frame of reference, and therefore the competitive context in which they themselves operate, purely in terms of their existing Nielsen category.

In recent years there has been a whole raft of packaging innovations, particularly in chilled food sectors. In the consumer's mind, chilled equals fresh equals added value. Yet the chiller cabinet remains largely the province of smaller manufacturers and retail brands. It probably took Heinz and Campbells at least a year to notice the very *existence* of chilled soups. They will have been too busy measuring their relative shares of the 'canned soup market'.

It has not just been happening in the chiller cabinet, but on the ambient shelves too. The UK pasta sauce market is now dominated by Unilever's Ragu and Mars's Dolmio, both of whose sales are primarily in glass jars. What happened to the erstwhile market leaders, Buitoni and Campbells? Still slugging it out in the 'canned pasta sauces market'. Not that I've got anything against cans, by the way. It is just an unfortunate coincidence that many of the most notable examples of packaging innovation in recent years happen to have been at the expense of cans.

To finish with a non-can example. Nabisco for years had a

snack brand called Twiglets. Available in boxes, it was bought by just about every household in Britain – but only once or twice a year, as one of a repertoire of 'nibbles' put out for parties, or for visiting relatives at Christmas. The physical pack format restricted the product's usage, which in turn restricted the brand's values in the consumer's mind. Yet all the while the *latent* values of Twiglets were capable of far broader appeal. All it took was to make the product available in foil bags suitable for eating 'on the hoof' and sales increased tenfold. (Incidentally, I once wrote a creative brief for a similar product and the draft which went to the client referred, thanks to a particularly unfortunate typing error, to the brand's suitability for eating 'on the roof'. The client felt this was taking niche marketing a little too far.)

What these cases illustrate is that physical packaging can have an enormously significant role in restricting or expanding a brand's potential.

Just as the successful brand owners of the past couple of decades have been those who have freed their brands from the constraints of particular *product* formulations and formats, so the successful brand owners of the future will be those who can free their brands from the constraints of particular *packaging* formats, giving them maximum flexibility to respond to changing consumer attitudes and changing technology.

And the most successful of these will be the ones who, whilst doing this, also think about what their physical packaging design *communicates* about the brand in question. About what its shape says. About what its material qualities and textures say. The ones, in other words, who think holistically about packaging as the embodiment of their brand's identity.

SUMMARY

1. 'Total Branding' is a new approach to packaging design as a marketing tool. It demands that the *whole pack*, not just the logo, should be regarded as the brand's identity. The whole pack should be used deliberately and actively to communicate brand values, not just product features.

2. Any pack design is capable, in its most passive mode, of absorbing meanings and values from other sources, even if these are not intrinsic to the design itself. Total Branding is about increasing the symbolic power of pack design by making it work harder, more actively, to communicate the right values rather than leaving it to time and chance.

3. It is important, in doing this, to understand the distinction between *product* values and *brand* values. The latter will, by definition, be bigger, richer, more unique and more enduring than the former.

4. Total Branding is about the total visual appearance of a pack, including its shape and structure.

5. Beyond this, it should also embrace the sense of touch – arguably the last great undiscovered marketing tool.

6. A brand's identity should never be locked in stone. Brands are living entities, and brand managements should be ready to embrace new visions, new structures, new shapes and new textures in response to changing consumer attitudes and changing technology – but always staying true to the brand's core values.

3

HOW IT WORKS

OF TWINKIES AND LOGO-LOUTS

The key principle of Total Branding is that the brand identity is the whole pack, not just the logo. Materials, texture, shape, graphics, colour, typography – every aspect of the pack should contribute to branding, ie to the communication of distinctive brand values.

And design will do this more effectively if it is based on a strong *idea*.

This is by no means as obvious as it sounds. The necessity for a strong idea has been a commonplace of thinking about advertising for many years. A good advertising campaign is expected to have a good idea at its heart. Agencies and clients alike, when discussing advertising proposals, will focus most of their attention on the strength or otherwise of this core idea.

As David Ogilvy once said, 'It takes a big idea to get the attention of consumers and get them to buy your product.'

Yet in the packaging design world, the importance of a strong and relevant idea is by no means universally accepted. Indeed, some of the leading design consultancies on both sides of the Atlantic are headed by creative directors who do not believe in ideas; who, in certain cases, wouldn't recognize an idea if it bit them on the bottom.

The opponents of ideas – and they are legion – can be divided into two camps: the Twinkies and the Logo-louts.

The Twinkies believe that craft and aesthetics are all that

matters. Principally British (though occasionally Dutch or French) they are the purveyors of restrained good taste and understated minimalism. At its best, their work is elegant in the extreme, and it tends to do very well in creative award schemes. Occasionally the personality such work exudes (quietly confident, stylish but slightly cold and aloof) happens to fit that of the brand to which it is applied, and on those occasions it can prove to be effective in the marketplace. But as often as not, such work is wholly inappropriate for the brands it adorns, and it all ends in tears.

The Logo-louts (often American, but with a fair smattering of British, French and Italian practitioners thrown in) are far more robust in their approach. Worshippers at the shrine of shelf-impact, they go in for bold graphics, bright colours and giant logos. As with the Twinkies, their work may or may not be a good match for the particular personalities of the brands on which they are working, but at least it sticks out like the proverbial dog's appendages. Or does so until you get a whole category (confectionery, for example) in which the Logo-louts have run amok, in which case their strident clamourings tend to cancel one another out.

What unites the Twinkies and the Logo-louts, despite the enormous differences in their creative output, is their lack of interest in ideas.

To be sure, they will talk of their work in terms of design *concepts*, but they use the word in so woolly and inaccurate a fashion as to be guilty of language abuse on a scale unmatched since 'value' became a synonym for 'cheap'.

When designers (be they Twinkies or Logo-louts) talk about a 'concept' what they invariably mean is 'a visual on a board'. If there are three visuals, there are three 'concepts'; six visuals equals six 'concepts'; and so on.

In truth, of course – or at least in the true sense of the word 'concept' – six visuals may contain six concepts, or else two concepts each executed in three different ways, or one concept executed in six different ways. Or (as is all too often the case) no concept at all.

The Twinkies and the Logo-louts are in this respect the same: they respond to a design brief by going straight to executional details. They often don't actually have 'concepts'. Or, worse, they think that a particular style of execution *is* a concept.

This is one of the reasons why design is often thought of as superficial; why the very word 'design' has become, in certain quarters, a byword for shallowness. Much that goes by the name of design *is* shallow – all surface, no substance; all style, no content.

But it doesn't have to be that way.

THE ROLE OF IDEAS IN PACKAGING DESIGN

The need for a real idea (I will keep on using this word, as 'concept' has become so devalued) stems directly from the need for packaging design to communicate brand values.

At the heart of any brand's value system is its *proposition*, or the essence of what it offers to the consumer. Rosser Reeves' USP, or Unique Selling Proposition, is now thought by some marketeers to be old hat. And indeed the belief that a brand's USP has to be a *rational* offer has long been superseded by subtler approaches. In UK advertising, Bartle Bogle Hegarty (the agency responsible for much of the most admired – and successful – advertising over the last decade) now talks about a brand's ESP, or Emotional Selling Proposition.

But the core argument – that every brand has or should have a particular *proposition* to put to the consumer – remains valid, be that proposition rational or emotional or a mixture of the two.

If this is the case, then surely one of the key tasks of the packaging designer (no less than the advertiser) is to communicate that proposition. And I am convinced that a pack design which has a strong and relevant idea at its heart will communicate that proposition quicker, more actively, and therefore more effectively, than one which hasn't.

So what do I mean by an 'idea' in packaging design? Let's look at a few examples.

Britvic have a brand in the UK soft drinks market called Tango. Its core product proposition is 'the taste hit of real oranges', supported by the fact that the product actually contains whole fruit juice. So Mark Wickens came up with the idea of a ring-pull opening an orange itself as the quickest way of communicating that proposition visually. For years, Tango cans had sported a copyline on the front face saying 'Made with whole fruit', yet even the brand's most loyal drinkers had turned out in research to be unaware of this fact (consumers don't read words on packs). It needed a visual idea to communicate effectively.

Terry's of York (until recently a subsidiary of United Biscuits, now part of Kraft Jacob Suchard) have a brand called Pyramint (see Plate 18). Its proposition is 'exotic indulgence' and every facet of the brand's presentation – product shape, packaging format, graphics, even the brand name – was created around the core idea of a pyramid to symbolize and communicate the 'exotic indulgence' proposition. The challenge which Terry's faced recently was to hang onto that idea even though the product itself was being developed into a 'countline' format (four pyramids joined together to make a bar). In this case, the idea of pyramids is absolutely fundamental to the brand's identity, and the new packaging has been successful largely because it managed graphically to retain the idea of pyramids even though the pack structure is no longer pyramid-shaped.

Or let's look again at the example of Gales Honey. That brand's proposition (admittedly a somewhat generic proposition, but market leaders are often those who have succeeded in making the generic their own) is 'the definitive pure and natural honey'. The idea of making the whole pack resemble a glass beehive stems directly from – and communicates directly to the consumer – that proposition.

If an idea is big enough, it can work across a wide range of different products from the same brand. In creating Tomy's 'Big Fun' brand of toys for toddlers, we were dealing with a range of literally hundreds of different toys, each with its own specific features and attractions (see Plate 19). What united them all was the fact that all of Tomy's toys have *lots* of features and attractions. They all *do* a lot, and Tomy pride themselves on packing more play-value (and, by extension, more learning-value) into their toys than can be found in any of their competitors' equivalents.

The brand's overall proposition is 'Learning through fun', which led to the idea of a visual 'alphabet of activity' to communicate it. The designer, Simon Coker, created a wide-ranging but controlled 'alphabet' of graphic symbols based on question marks, arrows, exclamation marks, musical notation and so on, a unique and distinctive visual language from which particular symbols could be selected and deployed to highlight the features of individual products, leading the consumer in each case via an 'equals' sign to the particular product name and descriptor.

This is an idea which is big enough to work on several levels at once. It had to be. It had to appeal to (and be understood by) adults and children alike. It had to transcend language barriers (the brand is pan-European). It had to work across a wide variety of different physical pack formats. It had to communicate the specific benefits of hundreds of different specific products. Yet it had to give the brand a coherent overall identity.

It does all of this not via spurious or irrelevant graphics but via a big idea which communicates the brand's proposition: it uses the visual language of learning in a fun way.

THE ROLE OF EXECUTION, OR STYLE

If the role of an idea in packaging design is to communicate the brand's proposition, the role of execution, or style, is to bring to life the brand's *personality*.

An idea can be executed in any number of different styles. The ring-pull opening the fruit on the Tango can, for example, could have been executed as a gentle water-colour illustration in quiet pastel colours. Or in a highly calligraphic manner, using carefully considered but apparently loose brush-strokes. Or photographically. Or as an oil painting.

For too many designers – and even some clients – such choices are driven by considerations of design fashion. Who is the 'hottest' illustrator at the moment? What will make it look 'modern'?

For too many clients – and even some designers – such choices are driven by considerations of category norms. What do packs in this market normally look like? What will make it look like all the rest?

In truth, all such considerations are – or should be – of secondary importance at best, if not completely irrelevant. The main factor driving the choice of a particular executional style should be the personality, or character, of the brand in question.

In the case of Tango, the brand's personality was in the process of transformation. It had become rather characterless over the years, but sensitive consumer research (of which more in Chapter 7) had guided us to a desired brand personality which would be youthful, irreverent, exuberant, British (in opposition to the overt American-ness of Coke and Pepsi and the most recently launched direct competitor Sunkist), and with a touch of 'street-cred' about it (see Plate 15).

It was that personality which dictated the way in which the 'ring-pull opening the fruit' idea was executed – vibrant colours against a black background, with the original illustrations being digitized and retouched to echo the visual language of video-games.

The key criterion in developing the final execution was not 'do we like it?' but 'does it communicate the right brand personality?'

Just as the core idea should be unique and true to the brand's proposition, so the style in which it is executed should be unique and true to the brand's personality.

TOTAL BRANDING: A QUICK TEST

Very few pack designs actually manage to achieve this degree of Total Branding. There is a simple test for whether it has been achieved or not. Cover up the logo and ask yourself honestly (or even better, ask your consumers via qualitative research) the four key questions:

- What proposition is being communicated?
- Is it distinctive and motivating in the competitive context?
- What personality does this brand have (ie what would be its characteristics if it literally came to life as a person)?
- Is this distinctive and motivating in the competitive context?

Depending on the answers to these questions, it should be obvious what the brand is, even with the logo covered up.

Why do so many pack designs fail this test? The reason, I think, is partly to do with lack of ambition – or at least different ambitions. Neither the Twinkies nor the Logo-louts even *try* to achieve the sort of totally branded communication

I've been describing. And their clients don't insist on it because they are themselves unsure about what packaging design can and cannot achieve.

But clients *should* be insisting on it. They should expect their packs to work as hard as possible at communicating their brand values. As Julian Behaeghel (the head of Design Board in Brussels, and the founder-president of the Packaging Design Association of Europe) has said, 'Communication is the function that is most under-used or badly used in packaging.' This is a terrible indictment of the packaging design business because, if you take away communication, what are you left with? At best, mere identification and/or prettification. Packs which either 'whisper sweet nothings' (the Twinkies) or else are 'full of sound and fury – signifying nothing' (the Logo-louts). Packs which look like other packs. Packs which do not truly belong to – and which therefore cannot *contribute* to – their brands.

BRAND PERSONALITY REVISITED

I want to dwell on this concept of 'brand personality' for a moment because I suspect one of the reasons for packaging design's frequent failure in this area has to do with confusion over the term itself. And this – perhaps surprisingly – is as true in the client community as it is among designers.

Most client briefs will include some reference to their brand's personality, or character, but it is astonishing how often a brief will describe a brand's personality in terms such as 'great tasting', 'effective', 'quality' or 'value for money', terms which are not personality attributes at all, and which are of next to no help to a designer trying to bring the brand's personality to life. It is in any case quite beyond the powers of packaging design alone to communicate 'value for money'. By definition, whether something is or is not 'value for money' is a consumer judgement which has price as its key variable. When a client writes 'value for money' in a brief, what he usually means is 'this brand is sold at a relatively low price-point, so don't make it look too expensive'. This merely compounds the confusion – surely you achieve value for money by making something look *more* expensive than the price-tag says it is?

In any case, such terms have no place in a definition of a brand's personality. To be useful – to inspire effective work from the designer – a brand personality statement should be an exercise in anthropomorphism. It should consciously (as consumers do, unconsciously) ascribe human characteristics to the brand in question, whilst taking especial care to ensure that it is the personality of the *brand* that is being described, not – as so often happens – the personality of the target consumer.

Is the brand male or female? Young or old? Technocrat, nurse or bank manager? Introvert or extrovert? Puritan or hedonist?

The more thorough and particular the definition of the brand personality in the brief, the better the chance that an expert packaging designer will be able to bring that personality to life in the design. Mind you, the Twinkies and the Logo-louts still wouldn't know what you were talking about!

THE FRAME OF REFERENCE: CATEGORY EQUITIES

So far in this chapter I have implied that brand values are all. That packaging design should be driven solely by the brand's proposition (from which the core idea should stem) and its personality (which should govern execution, or style). In practice, of course, these are not quite the only considerations.

Nobody designs (or buys) a brand in a vacuum. Brands exist in particular competitive repertoires, and these act as the 'frame of reference' within which each brand operates. Often, these repertoires will have developed over the years – whether by accident or design – particular visual languages, or category equities. And these impose certain constraints within which the communication of our own distinctive brand values must take place. Ignore too many of these category equities, move too far away from the established visual language, and you run the risk that you will have moved outside of the consumer's frame of reference. Your brand will simply be overlooked because it no longer 'belongs to the set'.

That said, there are two important points to make here. First, the frame of reference itself needs to be defined with great care. In most cases, there are at least three *potential* frames of reference to consider. There is the categorization used by the brand owner (usually corresponding to a Nielsen or AGB or Stats MR category). There is the categorization imposed by retailers – which is often a different one – in terms of the physical location of the brand on its fixtures. And then there is the frame of reference in the consumer's mind, which may very well be comprised using quite different dimensions from those used by the manufacturer or the retailer.

For example, the Five Alive brand from Coca-Cola (see Plate 20) is technically a 'juice-drink' (contains at least 5 per cent but less than 100 per cent juice) and is monitored against other 'juice-drinks'. Most retailers, however, pay little attention in merchandising to this distinction between juice-drinks and juices. Their fixture layouts are dictated by pack format, thus creating a frame of reference at point-of-sale of 'drinks in one-litre Tetrapaks'. In the consumer's mind, meanwhile, the frame of reference is much broader. Five Alive is one of a large number of loosely defined 'juices' in a repertoire which includes juices and juice-drinks, ambient and chilled, in a wide variety of pack formats. Depending on which frame of reference you consider, different category equities will need to be borne in mind.

Which brings me onto my second point on this subject. Such equities, or category norms, should not be used as a straitjacket if they get in the way of communicating distinctive brand values. There is no point in having a pack design which simply looks like all the rest. Just enough of the category's visual language should be used to ensure the brand is situated in the correct frame of reference – and no more. How much is 'enough' is something which needs to be carefully and sensitively researched. As a general rule, 'enough' turns out to be about half as much as the brand manager originally thinks!

But *some* deference to category norms is usually necessary. This is because of the human tendency to deal in stereotypes and instant classifications. As Abraham Maslow pointed out in *Motivation and Personality*: 'We tend to perceive things more easily as representatives of categories than in their own right, as unique and idiosyncratic.'

Maslow drew a distinction between what he called 'true perception' and 'categorized perception'. He might easily have had the modern supermarket environment in mind when he wrote that 'true perception, which would encompass the object as unique, play over all of it, soak it in, and understand it, would obviously take infinitely more time than the fraction of a second that is all that is necessary for labelling and cataloguing'.

In the modern supermarket, with its almost unbearable overload of visual stimuli, a fraction of a second is all a brand initially gets. If it is to use that fraction of a second to attract further attention, it must first announce itself in terms of categorized perception – what kind of thing it is.

A CAUTIONARY TALE

Some years ago, when I was Planning Director of Michael Peters & Partners, I learned the hard way about what can happen if necessary category norms are overlooked.

We had been briefed by Wall's to redesign the packaging of their traditional sausages. Consumer research had shown that the brand was a victim of its own success, having become so ubiquitous that consumers increasingly saw it as an impersonal, mass-produced, highly processed food, but perhaps with insufficient attention to quality of ingredients. This was unfair, as quality had always been of paramount concern at Wall's, as at all Unilever companies. Our brief was to endow the brand with some of the values of the traditional High Street butcher – an expert specialist, with a care for quality, a respect for tradition and a cheerful personality.

A design was produced to this brief. Against a royal blue background, there was an illustration of a jolly-looking butcher proffering a plateful of plump sausages; more sausages were illustrated hanging on hooks behind him; and the variant descriptors ('8 Pork and Beef Chipolatas' or whatever) were rendered in a fairly elaborate and traditional-looking typeface.

It sailed through qualitative research, having apparently met the brief perfectly, and it was with great confidence on the part of client and consultancy alike that the brand was duly relaunched in its new livery.

Sales dropped by over 30 per cent virtually overnight.

After exhaustive analysis to find out what had gone wrong, the vital error was pinpointed. We had broken a key 'category equity' of sausage packaging, namely that at least part of the main display-face should be transparent, showing the sausages within. Our design had covered the whole of the front face. The back and sides had been left transparent, because we knew that consumers demanded the reassurance of seeing the sausages themselves before they would buy. But to get to this point, they had first to pick the pack up. And whilst this had not suggested itself as a problem in qualitative research, in the real world alarming numbers of consumers were simply not getting that far.

In that vital split-second scan of the chiller cabinet, the sausage-seeking consumer was quite literally overlooking the Wall's packs. They said 'sausages' sure enough, and once spotted they communicated that these were indeed the best of sausages. But at a glance they did not *look* like sausage packs, and so the tastefully designed and strategically sound graphics never got a chance to work.

The solution was easy once the problem had been identified. The artwork was simply 'shrunk' to leave a transparent border around the graphics through which the sausages could be seen. Now it looked – at a glance – like a sausage pack; sales recovered and indeed, as predicted from the qualitative research, grew.

Category equities, by definition, will differ from category to category. And finding out which are the important ones, and which can safely be ignored, can be a difficult task. Conventional qualitative research is not always enough, as the Wall's example showed us. In that particular case, it took a research technique based on briefed shopping trips to uncover the real issue.

We'll look at research in more detail in the following chapters. For the moment, suffice it to say that one of the key issues that should be researched, ideally before creative work even starts, is this question of visual category norms.

Wally Olins wrote that 'breaking the visual generic demands courage and imagination. It also probably helps to be a bit ignorant, too.' Yes, but not *too* ignorant!

The trick, of course, is to strike the right balance: to obey enough of the 'rules' of a given category as to place the brand in the right frame of reference, but not to let those rules prevent you from having a big idea to communicate the brand's distinctive proposition, nor an original style of execution to communicate the brand's distinctive personality.

As the psychologist William James once wrote: 'The first thing the intellect does with an object is to class it along with something else. But any object that is important to us and awakens our devotion feels to us also as if it must be sui generis and unique.'

Categorized perception, and true perception – packaging design, if it is to be effective, must be rewarding on both levels.

BRAND EQUITIES

When redesigning established brands, there is another set of 'rules' to bear in mind – the visual equities built up over time by the brand itself.

The bigger the brand, and the longer it has been established, the more likely it is that certain visual features of its existing packaging will have imprinted themselves in consumers' minds.

Again, though, the trick is to work out which are the truly important equities, and which can safely be abandoned.

After all, the very fact that the brand is being redesigned suggests that all is not perfect with the current packaging. (We will ignore here those redesign projects which are commissioned for no wiser a reason than a new brand manager wanting to 'make his or her mark', and assume that there is some genuine commercial reason for the move.) And you can't move forward without leaving something behind.

When it comes to deciding which brand equities to retain, however, most brand managers again tend to err on the side of conservatism.

All too many briefs call for a fundamental repositioning of a brand – whether it is to appeal to a new target market, or to communicate a change in proposition, or to reflect a new competitive context or whatever – and then go on to give a list of 'equities thou shalt not change' which embraces just about every last detail of the pack in question: the shape, the logo, the colourways, the main symbol or graphic device, the copyline – the list goes on.

'So', the design consultant is tempted to respond, 'you want us to bring about a significant consumer reappraisal of the brand by shifting the bar-code half a millimetre, is that right?'

Usually, most of the items on the initial equity list turn out to be utterly disposable. Most brands have accumulated a good deal of graphic clutter over the years, sometimes for good reasons lost in the mists of time, and sometimes for no reason beyond a particular designer's – or a particular brand manager's – whim.

Much, or even all, of this clutter may seem important to the present brand manager. He or she is terrified of 'throwing the baby out with the bath water' but cannot be sure which is which. So the brand manager gives everything the benefit of the doubt, and assumes it's all pure baby.

One of the reasons for this, of course, is that he or she sits staring at the pack in an office all day every day. Not surprisingly, the brand manager comes to know it rather intimately. More surprisingly – if perhaps forgivably – he or she credits consumers with having an equivalent degree of intimacy with the brand. This is despite the fact that the brand manager knows in his or her heart that even the most loyal 'heavy user' does not actually sit staring at the brand all day, that, on the contrary, it commands only a few seconds of the consumer's attention per day at best. But even acknowledging this, the problem remains – which is baby, and which is bath water?

Again, research has a role to play. There's actually a very simple (but surprisingly underused) research technique which can help here, and we'll look at this in Chapter 7.

But first it's worth looking in more detail at the very nature of brand equities. There is an important distinction which needs to be made here between *saliency* and *contribution.* The former has to do with identifying which visual equities – and with what strength – consumers remember and associate with the brand; the latter has to do with what such equities are actually saying about the brand in question.

SALIENCY AND CONTRIBUTION

In understanding the difference between saliency and contribution, it may be helpful to think back to the distinction we drew in Chapter 2 between passive and active design. Packaging design works in both modes: passively, it sits there over time absorbing meanings from other sources, whereas actively, it will (if it is any good) be communicating positive meanings of its own.

Sometimes a brand can have visual equities which are high in saliency – because they have been associated with the brand for a long time, and have 'passively' acquired significance – but low in contribution, in the sense that closer examination reveals little, if any, active communicative content.

The Heinz 'keystone' device (or 'tombstone', as it is sometimes irreverently called) is a case in point. It has been used as a border to the Heinz logo since time immemorial, and has sufficient saliency for consumers to notice its absence if you try to remove it. But as for what it is doing there in the first place – what it is supposed to say about Heinz – nobody knows. Certainly consumers cannot 'decode' it. It is simply *there.*

Such passive equities can often be quietly dropped without any lasting damage being done. Certainly, consumers will notice that something has changed (and usually in a redesign exercise you want them to notice change anyway – one of the reasons for redesigning in the first place is to stimulate a consumer reappraisal of the brand) but the removal of equities which never actively communicated anything is unlikely to be harmful so long as sufficient continuity is maintained for the brand still to be recognizable.

Of more interest are the active equities – those which are not only high in saliency but also in contribution. The paddle-steamer on a Southern Comfort label is both salient (ie people remember it, and would notice if it were missing) and contributory – it symbolizes the brand's origins in both geography and time, and is executed in a style which is richly evocative of the brand's personality (see Plate 21).

Visual equities do not have to be figurative to be active and meaningful. The 'dynamic curve' on a Coke can is a purely abstract graphic device, but it contributes a sense of movement and energy to the brand's values.

Colour can be an equity, and again (like all equities) it can be either active or passive.

Cadbury's purple is an active colour equity. High in saliency, it is also high in contribution, as purple (due in part to its historical rarity as a dye, and consequent associations with only the rich and powerful such as royal families and the

Roman Catholic Church) has connotations of luxury which are entirely appropriate for a brand whose core product is chocolate.

Conversely, the turquoise colour of a Heinz baked beans label is almost certainly a passive colour equity. It's turquoise because it's turquoise, but for no apparent reason. (In fairness to Heinz, I should mention that a colour psychologist once explained to me that turquoise is actually the perfect colour for Heinz baked beans, because it is at the opposite end of the colour spectrum from the orange colour of the beans themselves. When you blink after looking at any colour, the brain retains an after-image of the opposite colour, so the turquoise label – if you blink whilst looking at it – makes you think of beans. Personally, I'm not convinced.)

The important thing about visual equities is to understand them as they truly contribute. Not in the brand manager's mind, nor in the designer's, but in the mind of the consumer.

SUMMARY

1. At the heart of Total Branding is a strong *idea* to communicate the brand's proposition. How this idea is then *executed* should be driven, above all else, by the brand's personality.

2. A particular executional style is not, in itself, an idea.

3. The world of packaging design currently comprises two camps – the Twinkies (aesthetes who believe in elegant prettification) and the Logo-louts (vulgarians who put shelf-impact above all else). Neither camp uses packaging design to its maximum active potential. Both eschew ideas, both are executionally driven, and both betray an inadequate understanding of brand values.

4. Brand values are not quite the be-all and end-all. In order to project the right brand values, a pack must first overcome the hurdle of 'categorized perception'. It must use enough category equities to place itself, in the consumer's first glance, in the right frame of reference.

5. Beyond this, in the case of redesign projects, it is important to be sensitive to the visual equities which the brand itself may have built up over time. But it pays to understand the difference between *saliency* and *contribution* in assessing such equities.

Exudes French elegance

2. The real thing?

Think of the brand and you think of the pack

4. Beefy brand, beefy jar

5. *Early example of active design*

6. *The atomium is a potent symbol*
© The Procter and Gamble Company. Used with permission.

. In need of refreshment?

8. Passive packaging

. Clean, pure and modern

10. Actively communicates brand values

11. *The whole pack is the identity, not just the logo*

12. *A totally integrated brand*

13. *Form follows brand values*

14. *Tactile as well as visual*

5. *A strong and relevant graphic idea*

16. *Looks good and feels good*

17. *Success through packaging innovation*

18. *Exotic indulgence*

19. *Active design for active toys*

. Makes category equities its own

21. Replete with active equities

. Using advertising characters

23. Lacks the character of the advertising

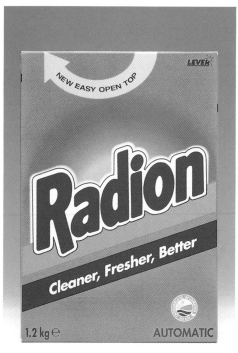

24. Consistent brand personality

25. Success through teamwork

4

THE BENEFITS OF TOTAL
BRANDING

STRATEGIC DISCIPLINE

Some of the benefits of Total Branding will, I hope, be self-evident by now. But achieving it can be so much more demanding than achieving an 'acceptable' pack design via the current 'standard' approach, that it seems to me to be worth spending a chapter examining in more detail the multiple benefits that make it worth the effort.

To start with, there's an indirect benefit – the strategic discipline which the quest for Total Branding imposes. There is nothing hit-or-miss about achieving Total Branding. It demands a thorough examination of a brand from a multiplicity of perspectives – the brand owner's vision, the competitive context, environmental considerations, the brand's history, the retail context, production considerations, and, most importantly of all, the consumer's perspective (for it is there, after all, in the consumer's mind, that the brand exists).

It demands strategic insight to then distil that understanding into a relevant and inspirational creative brief. It demands the intelligent application of creative judgement, aided by the sensitive use of consumer research. It demands considerable management skills and teamwork skills.

It is, in short, difficult and demanding to do well, and few marketeers can emerge from the experience without having found it in some way useful. If nothing else, they will understand their brands better at the end of it than they did at the beginning.

But that, as I say, is an indirect benefit. The direct benefits are to do with the effects on the performance of the brand itself.

TRIAL GENERATION

Total Branding helps a brand generate consumer trial. Consumers are attracted to a brand in the first place because it offers them a particular benefit (whether a rational or an emotional benefit, or a combination of the two) which they want.

They are not attracted to a brand merely because of product features, no matter how accurately represented on the pack. They are not attracted to a brand merely because the Twinkies have decorated it and it now looks pretty. Nor are they attracted to a brand merely because the Logo-louts have been to work and it screams off the shelf at them.

Product features, aesthetic appeal and shelf-impact are each important, of course. But they do not in themselves generate trial. What generates trial is the active communication of a motivating proposition, or benefit. And because benefit communication (via a strong *idea*) is at the heart of Total Branding it follows that, all else being equal, a totally branded pack will generate higher levels of trial than one which isn't.

Many marketeers rely on advertising alone to communicate their brand's proposition, and demand of packaging design only that it stands out and correctly identifies the brand at point-of-sale. This approach *can* work, of course, but it places an extraordinary degree of faith in the consumer's ability to (a) remember their advertising; and (b) recall it, proposition and all, when prompted merely by a logo or some other identification device at point-of-sale. It also presupposes that their advertising has achieved 100 per cent effective reach amongst their target market – a supposition which is either wishful thinking or hideously expensive to turn into reality, especially in these days of increasing media fragmentation.

And even for those brands which do have the luxury of enormous advertising budgets, why not use packaging design to communicate the brand's proposition all over again at point of sale? As James Pilditch said in *The Silent Salesman*:

'The package should say again all the things that have been said so expensively in advertising.' We will look in more detail at the relationship between advertising and design later in this chapter. For the moment, it is worth remembering that most brands do not have enormous advertising budgets – and even those which do, still have to sell in the periods between advertising bursts, when advertising awareness is decaying.

In these circumstances, for packaging design *not* to be used to communicate a brand's proposition seems to me to be almost wilfully negligent.

CONSUMER LOYALTY

If the active communication of a motivating proposition is the key to generating trial, it can also go a long way towards achieving repeat purchase (assuming, of course, that the product itself has been able to deliver against the proposition). But real consumer loyalty is harder to earn.

Professor Ehrenberg of the London Business School was among the first to prove what many marketeers and planners have since confirmed – in most markets, consumers are not loyal to one brand, but rather to a repertoire of five or six. Having first got onto that repertoire by stimulating trial, the real challenge for the marketeer is to maximize his or her share of each consumer's particular repertoire. Soft drinks marketeers have a compelling phrase for this when they talk about the battle for 'share of throat'.

Again, Total Branding has a role to play, but now it is no longer enough that the brand's proposition is actively communicated. When it comes to building loyalty, the more complex values of brand personality come to the fore.

Consumers will tend to be drawn most often to those brands which project the most appropriate personality. As we discussed in the previous chapter, consumers subconsciously imbue brands with human characteristics. Such anthropomorphism has long been a commonplace of clinical psychology, and its truth in relation to brands has been proven time and time again in qualitative research groups.

As consumers, we are seldom aware, at the conscious level, that we do this. Indeed, the first response of most sane people on being asked to describe what sort of person, say, Persil would be if he or she were to walk into the room, is usually one of blank-eyed incomprehension. But sensitively used projective techniques in research can tease out brand personalities of a richness and complexity that are often astonishing – not least to consumers themselves who had never before thought of Persil as the kind of brand that would read the *Daily Mail*, but who – now they come to think of it – are astounded by their absolute conviction that Persil could not possibly read any other newspaper!

The stronger the brand, the greater will be the consensus amongst its consumers regarding the characteristics of its personality – and the greater will be the richness and complexity of that personality once revealed.

What is also undeniable – again, because it has been proven in countless qualitative research groups – is the power of packaging design to create or to change a brand's personality.

This is not so surprising when you think about it. We all of us judge a book by its cover, and ascribe personalities to the people we meet based to a large extent on how they are dressed. If we think of packaging design as a brand's clothes, it is only natural that we judge that brand's personality at least partly on the basis of how it is dressed.

All of which makes it all the more astonishing that decisions about matters of executional style, in packaging design, are so often taken with little or no regard for the personality of the brand in question.

Total Branding, by contrast, makes considerations of brand personality of absolutely paramount importance in deciding on the appropriate executional style for a piece of packaging.

Here, it is worth stressing two points. The first is to say again that a brand's personality is often *not* the same as that of its target market. Some brands do, in effect, hold up a mirror to their consumers, saying 'buy me because I'm just like you'. Persil is arguably one such. But other brands project personalities which are quite different from their consumers. Ariel, for example, is bought mainly by women but has a decidedly masculine brand personality. It doesn't say 'buy me because I'm just like you' but 'buy me because I'm a scientist and I know my subject so you can rely on me'.

This brings me onto my second point. An appropriate brand

personality is not necessarily one which consumers *like* (though often it helps). Sometimes it can be more important that consumers *respect* it. Or *trust* it. Sometimes, a brand can even make a virtue out of personality traits which are not in themselves particularly likeable. Remy Martin, for example, is an out-and-out snob. BMW conforms to the teutonic stereotype of being utterly devoid of a sense of humour. Marks & Spencer is a middle-class male of the most pernickety variety. Yet these traits of brand personality not only fail to put us off buying that cognac, that car, those shirts – they are in each case part of the brand's appeal.

So asking consumers (whether for a blunt yes/no or via a more sophisticated five-point agree/disagree scale) how much they *like* a particular piece of packaging design can sometimes be entirely besides the point. But more of that in Chapter 8.

My point here is that projecting the right brand personality is one of the keys to building consumer loyalty. And that Total Branding – by making the pack work harder to communicate that personality – can be one of the marketeer's most powerful tools in achieving such loyalty.

BARRIERS TO COMPETITION

Another important benefit of the Total Branding approach to packaging design is the way in which it wrong-foots and excludes the competition, including Own Label imitations.

If your pack is merely a generic compendium of product features and irrelevant graphic devices (be they tastefully designed by Twinkies, or stridently designed by Logo-louts) there is little to stop the competition stealing your clothes. For the clothes themselves are insufficiently distinctive for anyone to notice the theft.

But if, by contrast, your pack is created around a strong *idea* to communicate your brand's particular proposition – and if, beyond this, that idea is then executed in a style particular to your brand's personality – then you will have created something unique, something that belongs exclusively to your brand, and would look wrong or out of place on anybody else's. If anybody else tried to copy it, the theft would be obvious, the imposter dismissed by consumers as a 'me-too', an 'also-ran'.

71

Other brands of toilet-cleaner can put a directional spout on their bottles, but no other brand can get close to Toilet Duck. Most brands of orange-flavoured soft drink have a picture of an orange somewhere on their packs, but it would be suicide for any other brand to try to 'do a Tango'. For any other brand of pre-school toys to try to mimic Tomy's distinctive visual alphabet would merely expose the fact that Tomy's toys *do* more, and therefore have more to say about themselves.

In each case, the pack design is the exclusive property of the brand because the brand owns the *idea* on which it is based. The lawyers say you can't own an idea. In packaging design, you can – not because of the law (though the law is now getting better at protecting design copyright, despite the notorious inability of lawyers to cope with anything that cannot be photocopied in black and white and kept in a file) but because overt rip-offs don't work, and the stronger the idea the more overt the rip-off if anybody tries it.

Even in the case of Own Label rip-offs (the one area in which design mimicry *has* sometimes worked) a strong idea can be a powerful deterrent. This is partly because an imitation would need to be more blatant, thus improving the brand owner's legal case in any 'passing-off' action. And – perhaps more importantly – imitations need to be almost subliminal to have the desired effect on consumers. The more blatant the imitation, the more it paradoxically calls attention to what it is *not*.

BRAND EXTENSION

Total Branding makes the process of brand extension both easier and more rewarding.

This is partly because it is a *strategic* approach to packaging design, and much of the strategic work done on the brand's core product(s) will provide a valuable strategic framework for later line extensions. And partly it is because Total Branding yields stronger visual equities which will work harder than a mere logo in effecting the transfer of brand values onto the new products being introduced.

Let us deal with each in turn.

Strategically, the Total Branding approach forces the distinction between product features and brand values. It is a marketing truism too often overlooked to say that a brand's values (even if they derive initially from a particular product) are bigger and more powerful than the product itself. So a brand can ultimately offer a range of products, not just one, provided always that those products are capable of sharing – and having perceived value added by – the same core brand values.

Al Ries and Jack Trout, in their seminal work *Positioning – The Battle for Your Mind*, exposed the dangers of indiscriminate line extension. They called it 'the free ride trap' and pointed out that 'a (brand) name is a rubber band ... the more you stretch it, the weaker it becomes.' This, of course, is true. Bearing in mind the point made earlier about brands living in consumers' minds, and how you can therefore line-extend only so far as the consumer will allow you to, it is obvious that the quickest way to kill a brand is to slap its logo indiscriminately on products which do not 'fit'. As Ries and Trout say, this kind of line extension merely educates the consumer to the knowledge that the brand name is nothing but a name. It destroys the brand's magic, taking away its personality and leaving behind not a brand but a 'bland'.

But Ries and Trout go too far when they assert that 'when a new product comes along it's almost always a mistake to hang a well-known name on it'. Try telling that to Lever Brothers or to Procter & Gamble, whose Persil and Ariel brands have moved effectively through four generations of product technology – from soap powders through synthetic detergents, through liquids to concentrates. Or to Kodak, whose 'visual imaging' expertise allows the same brand values to apply with equal relevance to all forms of camera film as well as to 'hardware' products like slide-projectors.

The trick, of course, is to make sure that all products in the range share the same core brand values.

Total Branding – by identifying and encapsulating these values from the outset – facilitates this process no end. Done properly, it maps out the product territories into which the brand can and cannot go.

Having helped in the definition of line extension strategy, Total Branding then makes line extension much easier from a design point of view. The Ariel 'atomium' is a powerful graphic idea which encapsulates and symbolizes that brand's 'scientifically advanced cleaning power' proposition. Applied to other scientifically advanced cleaning products, it is capable of working so much harder than a mere logo ever could. We have already seen how the 'visual alphabet of activity' created for Tomy's Big Fun brand facilitated line extension across literally hundreds of pre-school toy products. Tango's 'ring-pull opening the fruit' idea could easily – if Britvic so chose – be adapted to different opening mechanisms on different pack formats for other fruit-based products.

But most brands do not have a strong visual idea to help transfer their brand values onto new products; most have only a logo.

Interestingly, many of the brands which *do* have a good visual idea have derived that idea from advertising. One thinks of the Dulux dog, the Bisto kids (see Plate 22), the Andrex puppy, the Tetley tea-men, or Fred the Homepride flour-grader. All of these advertising properties have proven to be sufficiently enduring to feature eventually (albeit sometimes half-heartedly) on their brand's packaging. Arguably they should have been used earlier, and more strongly.

This brings me onto the next potential benefit of Total Branding.

SYNERGY WITH ADVERTISING

It has been a source of amazement to me for many years to see how many brands have advertising which says one thing to the consumer, whilst their packaging design says something completely different, if it is saying anything at all.

Surely, as the two primary vehicles for brand communication, the two should at least be driven by the same strategy? And in many cases, does it not make sense for them to share the same big idea to communicate the brand's proposition? The same executional style to convey the brand's personality?

I'm not suggesting that total synergy will always be the right answer. There are often good reasons for ascribing different roles to the two media so that they are mutually complementary rather than mutually reinforcing.

For example, advertising can sometimes quite properly be used to suggest a 'lifestyle context' for a brand – something which packaging design is ill-equipped to do. Conversely, the need to endow a brand with category authenticity – putting it in the right 'frame of reference' in terms of the categorized perception referred to earlier – is more of an issue at point-of-sale (and therefore a task for packaging design) than something which advertising necessarily needs to address.

There are other obvious differences. The visual contexts which each has to contend with are different – the competitive 'brandscape' and merchandising conditions in the case of design, the editorial environment and competitive ads in the case of advertising. Advertising can, depending on the medium, use time – for 'before-and-after' comparisons, for example – whereas packaging design can deal only with 'after'. Packaging is tactile in a way which advertising is not (you can touch the medium in which an ad appears, but you can't touch an ad). Advertising is a transient communication tool, capable of being changed at short notice, whereas packaging design is more 'permanent'.

But despite all these differences, the core tasks for each are actually the same: to communicate a motivating and distinctive proposition, and to do so in a way which endows the brand with the right personality. Given this, it is astonishing how seldom you see a brand whose advertising and packaging design appear to have been thought through together.

So often, a powerful idea will crop up in one or the other, but fail to be carried across, or an executional style will be developed in one, which perfectly captures the brand's personality, only to be ignored in the other.

For example, the brand personality of Mr Kipling cakes has for years been captured superbly on TV in the rich tones of voice-over artist Cyril Shaps. Is that tone-of-voice carried over in any way onto the brand's packaging design? No. Why not? Because you can't put a voice on a pack? Ah, but you can. That's what the typographer's art is all about (see Plate 23).

Some brands do manage to achieve the synergy I'm talking about, and their sales must surely benefit as a result. Lever's Radion brand, for example, lacks (in the purist sense) a big visual *idea*, but makes up for this in the strength of its executional style – sharp, day-glo graphics perfectly encapsulate the brand's powerful, zappy, 'in-yer face' personality, a style which is carried through consistently across both advertising and design (see Plate 24).

Sanatogen, the vitamins and minerals brand, exhibits the same sort of consistency; other examples include Monster Munch, the children's snack, or Silhouette, Johnson & Johnson's sanpro brand. Cigarettes and drinks brands often achieve high degrees of synergy between packs and ads, too, but for different reasons – legislation is so restrictive in terms of what advertising can say about the *products* that the focus of attention in advertising is forced onto the pack.

More and more marketeers, realizing the obvious benefits of pack-and-ad synergy, are these days working consciously to achieve it. Some try to do this by getting the same creative team to do both. Sadly, this seldom works, as the craft skills necessary to produce great packs are seldom to be found in advertising creatives, and vice versa. So what the wiser marketeers are starting to do is to get their ad agencies and their design consultancies to work more closely together. This has to make sense.

In truth, it doesn't matter where the big idea comes from, so long as both are working to the same strategy. The designers might come up with a big idea that can be made to work in advertising, or the ad agency might come up with a big idea that can become the heart of a pack design. Who cares where the idea comes from? (Actually, they both care, but the management of conflicting egos has always been an important skill in the marketeer's armoury!)

What Total Branding does is to increase your chances of achieving synergy at all. If there's a big idea in the brand's advertising, then the practitioner of Total Branding will seize on it and put it to work on pack. If there isn't, he or she will create one, and the astute marketeer will insist that it finds its way into the ads. The better ad agencies will have spotted it in any case, and will want to make use of it. The stronger and more visually relevant the pack, the more the creative team in the advertising agency will want to feature it in the commercial. In fact, true synergy is not so much about featuring the pack itself in advertising, as about featuring the same *idea*, and achieving the same executional style, or tone-of-voice.

But this is only possible if your packaging design is being developed along Total Branding lines. If not – if it's simply a logo and some irrelevant graphics – then all you'll have to put in the ads is a gratuitous pack-shot.

BRAND VALUES AND BRAND VALUE

The ultimate benefit of Total Branding, via all of the above, is a more valuable brand. It is remarkable that the value of brands has only recently become a topic for debate among chief executives, finance directors and city analysts. It is even more remarkable that the difficulty of measuring brand value (how do you measure something that is so intangible, it only exists in the minds of millions of consumers?) has so far resulted in most accountants giving it up as an impossible task.

Yet the real financial value of a strong brand is beyond doubt. Did Nestlé really pay £2.5 billion for Rowntree's chocolate factories? Or were they paying for the value of Kit-Kat, of Rolos, of Quality Street?

When the financial community places a value on companies such as Cadbury Schweppes, or Coca-Cola, or United Biscuits, what it is valuing is the potential future profit stream in each case. And what produces those profits? Their brands, of course. As Roland Jeannet of Johnson & Johnson succinctly put it: 'Brands produce more profits than mere products.'

Studies conducted by Peter Doyle, the Professor of Marketing at Warwick University, have demonstrated that brands with a 40 per cent market share generate three times the ROI of those with a market share of only 10 per cent. The stronger the brand, the bigger the profits. And since brands, as we have seen, only exist in the consumer's mind, there can be no denying the truth of Doyle's assertion that 'the value of a product is not what the producer puts in, but what a consumer gets out'. Or to put it another way, the manufacturer makes products, but the consumer buys brands – and pays for the added value.

The whole question of brand value was perhaps best summed up not by a marketeer at all, but by the French art critic Jean Bazaine who, in his *Notes on Contemporary Painting* observed that 'an object awakens our love just because it seems to be the bearer of powers that are greater than itself'.

That seems to me to be exactly how brands work. And Total Branding by design is arguably the most direct and effective way of imbuing a product with 'powers that are greater than itself' ... with real brand values – to enhance real brand value.

SUMMARY

1. The Total Branding approach yields enormous benefits, not least through the strategic discipline which the quest for Total Branding demands.

2. Because consumers are in the market primarily for *benefits* (be they rational or emotional), Total Branding – by communicating a brand's principal benefit via a strong idea – helps maximize trial.

3. Beyond this, by endowing the brand with a motivating and distinctive personality, it helps stimulate consumer loyalty.

4. Done properly, it discourages me-toos and imitations, because it results in an identity which is more ownable.

5. It facilitates relevant brand extension, both by clarifying the brand's core values, and by providing a vehicle much more powerful than a mere logo for the transfer of brand values onto other products.

6. Total Branding provides bigger opportunities for synergy with advertising and other communications tools, because a big idea can work across all media.

7. Through all of the above, Total Branding can increase the financial value of brands.

5

THE TOTAL BRANDING
TEAM

THE CLIENT TEAM

Achieving Total Branding requires, above all else, teamwork. It requires the bringing together of a team of specialists, all of whom will have their own perspectives, their own priorities and their own agendas, and getting them to work together towards the common goal.

Brand Management

In many ways, this is the core activity. Brand Management is, after all, at the heart of the process. The brand management team are 'the client', responsible for initiating a design project in the first place, for writing the initial brief, and then for driving the project and managing the team through to its successful conclusion.

Apart from the obvious marketing skills involved in knowing the brand and its competitive context inside out, and having a clear vision of where the brand is going, the brand management team need to bring several additional skills to bear on a packaging design project:

■ *motivation:* a good design team will find their own motivation, but it still helps to have a client who is a source of encouragement rather than constantly nit-picking!

■ *forward-planning:* achieving Total Branding takes time, so there's no point in briefing the design consultancy

83

three weeks before the date you've committed to have your new pack ready for the Sales Conference.

■ *Budget control:* the two key ingredients here are to be realistic, and to be honest with your design consultancy. Be realistic in setting the budget in the first place (so many brand managers 'know the cost of everything and the value of nothing' and buy design services purely on price – a decision which nearly always costs them more in the end). Be honest because most design consultancies will genuinely try hard to stay within your budget – but they can't do that if they don't know what it is!

■ *Self-restraint:* it is the job of the brand management team to give, or to withhold, approval, but not to end up art directing the pack themselves. If you find yourself doing your own art direction, then either your designers are incompetent, or you are overstepping the bounds of the contribution you should be making.

Market Research

If (as this whole book presupposes) the key task of packaging design is about communication, then it goes without saying that an understanding of the target market is fundamental. You can't communicate if you don't know who you're communicating with, or what they currently think.

Market research is therefore vital. These days, most advanced marketing companies will have in-house market research managers, usually employing a roster of outside qualitative and quantitative specialists. We will look at the role of research in packaging design in more detail later on.

Trade Marketing

In most markets, the growing power of the stronger retailers has led to manufacturers redefining the classical 'sales' function. A key aspect of a modern sales strategy is 'Trade Marketing'. It is about developing real partnerships with key retailers. And it has led to a fundamental change in the role of brand management (and, by extension, of their design consultancies). No longer is it safe, or even reasonable, to suppose that the retail trade will 'take what we give them'. They need to be consulted, and their views taken into account, on just about any proposed brand development of any significance, if it is to have the slightest chance of success. Often, indeed, they will have provided the initial prompt or impetus for the proposed brand development happening at all! The Trade Marketing team represent the views of these key retailers in the design development process.

Production

Because packaging design, unlike other forms of brand communication, is tangible – and because it has an intimate relationship with the product itself – it has to be physically produced in a way which meets a whole host of different criteria: materials specifications, print tolerances, health and safety considerations, tamper-evidence, filling-line speeds, environmental factors, cost-efficiency, pallet configurations, stability in transit ... the list goes on.

Again, manufacturers will have a team of experts in production and factory management whose role is to ensure that all key criteria are understood and satisfied.

THE DESIGN CONSULTANCY TEAM

Designers

The core creative skill, the hardest to define, and the most vital of all in achieving Total Branding. You can get all the other skills in place, get a clear understanding of the common goal, and go through the perfect process to get there ... but if you haven't got a highly creative design team to bring the brand to life with that elusive bit of magic, then the whole thing will have been a waste of time and effort.

Some marketing companies still employ in-house design teams, but that is becoming rarer for the simple and obvious reason that the most talented and creative designers hardly ever want to work in-house for a manufacturing company. They want to work for the best specialist design consultancies.

Account Management

That being the case, the brand management team is usually mirrored on the design consultancy side by an account management team.

There are some consultancies (Minale Tattersfield, for example) which eschew account managers and prefer instead to have designers do their own account management. I have to say I have never seen the sense in this. Good account management involves a level of understanding of marketing issues which it is not only rare for a designer to have, but also unreasonable to *expect* a designer to have. Moreover, it involves primarily left-brain skills (verbal and written presentation, logistics management, budget management) whereas it is mainly for their right-brain creative skills that designers are employed.

Of course, some designers are so prodigiously well-rounded that both hemispheres of their brains operate to the same high standards (my own creative partner, Mark Wickens, is one such, and in my days in advertising with Abbott Mead Vickers, Creative Director David Abbott was known to be the best account handler in the place) but in my experience such paragons are rare.

In his otherwise excellent book, *How to Run a Successful Multi-disciplinary Design Company*, Marcello Minale argues vehemently against account handlers 'coming between' client and designer. But nowhere does he explain how his way results in better or more effective designs being produced – only that it is the way to 'maximize profitability'. Unfortunately, Marcello doesn't say whether or not his designers take it in turns to staff reception and to clean the toilets on the same principle.

To be fair, though, Minale Tattersfield have produced a terrific body of effective design work over the years, so they must be doing something right.

But in my view, a better way to produce consistently effective packaging design is to leave designers free to concentrate mainly on designing, whilst the tasks of organizing meetings, understanding the client company, writing action reports, developing timing and budget plans, invoicing and all the other paraphernalia of managing the project and the business relationship are looked after by account handlers who are more skilled in these areas.

Planning

This is the newest, and most controversial, of the battery of skills you might nowadays expect a design consultancy to bring to the party.

First established over 25 years ago in UK advertising (BMP and JWT are widely credited with having 'invented' it more or less simultaneously) it was predicated on the principle that clients are often too close to their brands – and account handlers get to be too close to their clients – to have the insight which a more objective, consumer's-eye, viewpoint might provide.

So a new breed of Planner was introduced, as 'the voice of the consumer in the creative process'. Figure 5.1 shows the respective orientations of planners and account handlers. The advertising planner's principal tool was thus consumer research – but he or she differed from the client's market research manager in being much more closely and specifically oriented towards the creative product, namely advertising. To meet the specific needs of advertising development, a whole new raft of research techniques and methodologies were developed. And to cut a long story short, the underlying premise that this new Planning discipline would result in better creative briefs, which in turn would inspire better and more effective advertising (in BMP's memorable phrase, 'more right more often') has been proven beyond all reasonable doubt in the last 25 years.

Yet it is only in the last decade that the core principles of planning have been applied to packaging design. Indeed, when I was charged with introducing ad-agency-style planning into Michael Peters and Partners in 1986, I believe it was the first time a design consultancy had chosen to go down this path.

Fig. 5.1 *The complementary responsibilities of planners and account managers*

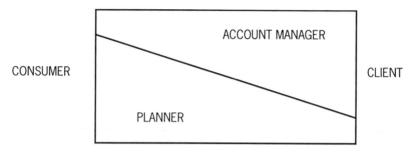

When my partners and I set up Wickens Tutt Southgate in 1989, we did so with planning as a fully integrated core discipline – 'design with planning as part of the package', as our launch ads said – and (though we still like to think we are ahead of the game in this respect) planning has now been taken up with varying degrees of enthusiasm by most of our key packaging design competitors.

As it did in advertising all those years ago, it is leading to new, and better, research techniques (and to the throwing out of some old but dud ones) in the quest to inspire more effective work via better briefs.

Artwork Production

The other key skill on the consultancy side is artwork production. This too has become a controversial area, but for different reasons. The advent of DAR (Digital Artwork Reproduction) via new technology is sounding the death-knell for traditional mechanical artwork. Digital artwork production is a hi-tech, highly specialized skill in its own right, and the world of packaging design consultancies is rapidly splitting into those who are rushing to embrace it, and those who are resisting it. The Luddites, as always in such battles, will be the losers. But that is not to say that those who are undiscriminating in their enthusiasm for DAR will necessarily win.

The key here is to use the new technology for all its advantages (faster repro and proofing, greater flexibility and more accurate print production at the end of the day) whilst retaining the craftsmanship, quality control and attention to detail that characterized the traditional methods at their best. In other words, anyone who can operate the technology can produce digital artwork. But it takes high-level design input from the original designer to produce *good* digital artwork.

THE FULL TEAM APPROACH

The direct relationship between client team and design consultancy team is illustrated in Figure 5.2. But the full team should ideally be bigger than this. For although design is at the heart of a brand's communications, it is only a part of a bigger process. The marketing mix is likely to include advertising, sales promotion, PR, sponsorship and, increasingly, Direct Marketing (or Relationship Marketing as many of its leading practitioners now prefer to call it). Ideally, all of these brand communication tools should be in harmony with one another.

Ultimately, of course, it is the role of the brand management team to ensure that this is the case. And it could be argued that the best way to ensure such harmony is achieved is to channel all communications through the brand management team, with no direct contact between the various external agencies who might be involved.

In my experience, however, the smartest clients (and the ones who get the most out of their agencies) are those who actively encourage their agencies to get together and share their thoughts (both strategic and creative) throughout the process. It's one thing for a design consultancy to be given a copy of the client's advertising strategy, for example, but quite another for them to meet the advertising agency and be taken through the agency's interpretation of that strategy – to be taken through the agency's thinking in detail, and to understand exactly why a campaign has been, or is being, developed along particular lines. By the same token, an ad agency which has been kept fully informed throughout the design development process will be much more likely to find imaginative uses for the design idea in its own advertising development than one which has simply had a pack foisted on it as a *fait accompli* at the end of a process from which it has been kept at arm's length.

Figure 5.2 *The client/design consultancy relationship*

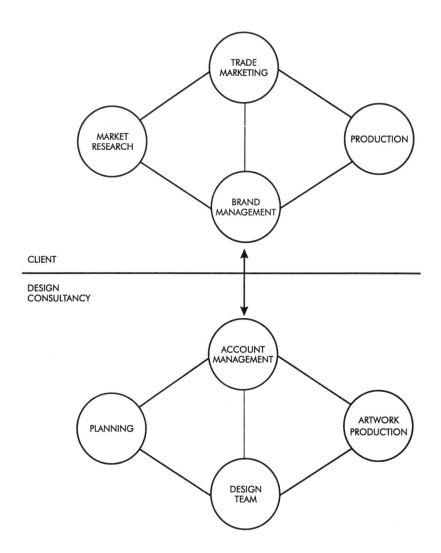

No client in my experience has understood this better than Tony Hillyer, formerly the Marketing Director of Britvic and, at the time of writing, Marketing Director of Littlewoods Pools. Tony was our first client on Tango – a project which was remarkable, among other things, for the close collaboration which Tony encouraged between ourselves and the ad agency, Howell Henry Chaldecott Lury.

Both agencies were given the same initial brief, which consisted largely of a SWOT analysis on Tango as it then stood, together with a statement of overall marketing objectives. Thereafter, we both assisted in the commissioning of fresh consumer research to investigate the brand's communications in terms of our respective specialisms in more detail. We shared those pieces of research, attending one another's debriefs and jointly discussing the resulting findings. We shared our internal creative briefs with each other, both as a cross-check and as a potential source of mutual inspiration. And for the same reasons, we shared creative work-in-progress. Tony and his brand manager, David Dean, were present at many of these meetings, but by no means all of them. With the clients' blessing, we were free to call in HHCL at any time, and vice versa.

The results speak for themselves. Howell Henry's 'You know when you've been Tango'd' campaign won a raft of advertising awards, our new packs won a raft of design awards and – most importantly of all, obviously – Tango put on significant share gains despite the recent arrival of a heavyweight, and heavily supported, new direct competitor called Sunkist.

The new Tango team at Britvic, headed up by David Atter, has continued this approach. HHCL, Wickens Tutt Southgate and the Britvic people continue to work in close harmony (any member of the team can call a full-team meeting at any time, for example) and I confidently expect Tango to go from strength to strength for many years to come.

Another enlightened client is Gossard (see Plate 25). When, after 25 years, the UK licence to market Wonderbra was taken away from Gossard and given to key competitors Playtex, the Gossard marketing team (John Hall, Mark Pilkington and Laura Cannon) assembled a multi-agency task force to launch their new brand, the Ultrabra. For the latter half of 1993, and in conditions of the utmost secrecy, Abbott Mead Vickers (advertising), Wickens Tutt Southgate (design), Momentum (Sales Promotion) and Janet Hurton (PR) met and shared work-in-progress, resulting in what must have been one of the most fully coordinated new brand launches ever (certainly in that market) when Ultrabra was launched on 1 January

1994. With the withdrawal of the Wonderbra licence, Gossard had lost 40 per cent of total brand volume at a stroke. Ultrabra not only replaced the whole of that lost volume, but in its first half-year actually increased Gossard's plung-bra sales by 50 per cent. (And this at a time when the 'grunge' fashion had supposedly made cleavages redundant!)

I have no doubt that in both of the above examples the success which was achieved was due in no small measure to the depth of direct interaction between the various agencies. Figure 5.3 illustrates this 'full-team' approach.

Figure 5.3 *The 'full team' approach*

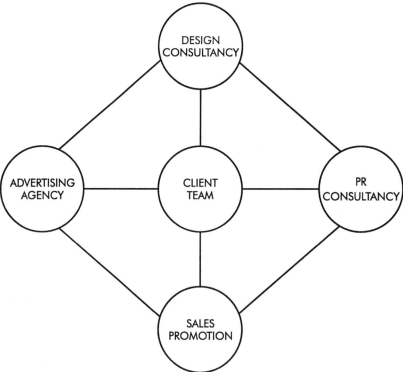

(NB: Depending on the nature of the client's business other specialisms such as Direct Marketing may be added.)

ONE-STOP SHOPPING?

Does this imply that clients should go one step further, and seek full team interaction by buying all of their agency services under one roof (what used to be called 'one-stop shopping' but is increasingly presented as 'through-the-line')? No, for the same reason it is not a good idea for clients to have creative services in-house. The best people in each field want to work for the best specialists in that field. Logically, there is no reason why a single agency should not become the best in *all* fields, but in practice I don't believe it will ever happen. One type of service is bound to be dominant, either in the agency's culture or in the eyes of the outside world. It is my firm belief that an agency can only be truly great at (or become famous for being great at, which eventually amounts to the same thing) one craft, so it will never attract the best people in the others.

So it's down to the client brand management team to select the best mix of specialists – and then get them to play as a team.

A model of 'one-stop shopping' which *might* have a future is the new type of 'marketing agency' which houses planners and account handlers but has no creative services in-house. Such an agency has no dominant creative culture because it has no creative culture at all. It is theoretically able to offer truly impartial advice on the whole marketing mix, calling on and managing specialist creative agencies or freelancers in the various different disciplines as appropriate.

But is this not the natural role of the client's marketing management? And is not marketing too central a corporate function to be 'outsourced' in this way except by the smallest of client companies?

There will always be a role for the individual marketing consultant, and the new type of marketing agency is the same thing on a slightly bigger scale. But I would be most surprised were they to become a significant force. At the time of writing, even The Added Value Company (arguably the most successful of the new-style marketing agencies) seems to be abandoning this positioning by bolting on a number of in-house creative services. The ad agency Leo Burnetts recently relaunched itself as a 'marketing agency' but it turned out only to be another way of dressing up 'one-stop shopping' with the addition of a discrete brand strategy unit to the usual menu of creative services. Its brand strategy unit may well attract some of the brightest and broadest strategic thinkers (if only because of the well-earned reputation of its founder, Simon Broadbent). But for all the reasons discussed earlier, the best creatives (in *any* discipline) are unlikely to want to work for a 'one-stop shop'.

So the central role of marketing – the management and coordination of the best teams of specialists in all the marketing services – will I believe remain on the client side, with the brand management and/or category management teams.

What *is* changing in this respect is the balance between the different marketing services. The position of the advertising agency as the 'lead' agency in the marketing mix is being challenged as never before. This, I think, is due to a combination of factors: the growing strategic orientation of agencies in design, direct marketing, sales promotion and PR; the growing ability of such agencies to demonstrate the cost-effectiveness of their contributions; and a backlash against some of the failings of advertising agencies (creative self-indulgence, complacency, lousy cost control – that sort of thing) over the past decade or so.

The marketing mix is now truly a mix, where once it was advertising plus a bit of below-the-line stuff. The fact that the mix is these days more balanced makes true teamwork more difficult in some ways – but it also makes it all the more important to achieve it.

SUMMARY

1. Total Branding requires teamwork of a high order. The biggest challenge facing brand management is to bring a wide range of specialists together and to get them to play as a team.

2. Within the client organization, research managers, sales and trade marketing people and production staff all have crucial roles to play at different stages in the process.

3. As well as designers, most design consultancies these days have specialists in account management, planning and artwork production. The latter field is seeing rapid technological advances, with enormous potential benefits, but also with significant risks if abused.

4. Beyond the client/design consultancy team, the full team on a Total Branding project should include the agencies responsible for all other key aspects of the marketing mix. And it pays to encourage those agencies to interact as much as possible.

5. But this is not an argument for 'through-the-line' or 'one-stop' shops. The best people in all marketing services want to work for the best specialists in their chosen field.

6. These days, the marketing mix is much more balanced, which makes cross-disciplinary teamwork all the more important.

6

GETTING GOING

THE IDEAL CLIENT BRIEF

B riefing a design consultancy – or any marketing services agency, come to that – is always tricky. How much information should you put in the brief? Do you cram in everything you can think of, on the grounds that they will ignore what they don't need but at least nothing vital will be missing? Or do you keep it short and sharp, on the grounds that if they want more information they can always ask? How directive should you be? Should the brief tell them exactly what you want, or merely draw the broad parameters to which they must keep, leaving a fair degree of freedom within these bounds?

Unfortunately, there are no easy answers to these questions as they depend on the nature of the project, and to some extent on the nature of the consultancy being briefed.

In the case of an NPD project, for example, the ideal brief will vary depending on whether or not the product itself has yet been finalized. And the ideal brief for an agency with a strong planning capability will be very different from one destined for an agency without this capacity.

So what follows is inevitably a rather subjective and generalized view. But I do believe it is possible to define some basic principles in terms of what an ideal brief should contain, and what it should not.

Project Scope

A brief should ideally start with a definition of the task and its scope. Creating a new brand? Line extension to an existing brand? Repositioning? Relaunch? The brief should say which, and should outline broadly why this project is being undertaken. It should then define the products involved (assuming more than one) and the number and nature of different individual items or s.k.u.s. (stock-keeping units). Finally it should state whether the project calls purely for graphic design on existing packaging structures, or whether there is scope for 3D structural design as well.

Background

This should be kept fairly succinct, detailing the brand or project history only insofar as that history has a direct relevance to, and bearing on, the task in hand, and finishing with a short summary of the brand's (or project's, in the case of a new brand development programme) current situation.

Marketing Objectives

This is the most important part of the brief, in that this is the only part that should be regarded by the design consultancy as absolutely sacrosanct. Everything else may or may not be subject to challenge, debate or improvement during the course of the dialogue you are now entering into. But the overall marketing objectives should be set in stone. They are the goals towards which the whole project should be geared.

These should be relatively 'high-level' objectives, concerned with dimensions such as market share, annual sales value, household penetration, net contribution or the like.

I stress this because it is easy to fall into the trap of setting so-called marketing objectives which in reality belong to a lower level in the hierarchy of objectives. Building brand awareness, for example, is a task best suited to advertising and/or PR; other marketing tools can have comparatively little impact on this dimension. As such, a target level for brand awareness should be an advertising or PR objective rather than an overall marketing objective. By the same token, achieving high shelf standout and differentiation at point-of-sale are tasks for design, and should therefore be considered as potential design objectives. The overall marketing objectives should be bigger and broader in scope, ideally being objectives to which all or most of the weapons in the marketing armoury can contribute in their different ways.

The other thing to say about these objectives (and forgive me for stating the obvious here, but you would be surprised how many client briefs are deficient in this regard) is that they should conform to the SMART principle, which is to say they should be:

- Specific

- Measurable

- Achievable

- Realistic

- Time-defined.

Brand SWOT Analysis

In the case of an existing brand, it is useful at this point to include the marketing team's analysis of the brand's current Strengths, Weaknesses, Opportunities and Threats. Again, these should be defined at a reasonably high level, giving the 'big picture' rather than getting into minor or temporary detail: the observation that a brand suffers from unusually low levels of impulse purchase might, for example, be a useful weakness to highlight, whereas the fact that it suffered a share-dip in the Border TV area in the last Nielsen period, though interesting, is going into too much detail to be useful here.

Design Objectives

These should obviously relate to, and indeed be driven by, the overall marketing objectives, but now focusing on those tasks which packaging design in particular needs to achieve.

It should go without saying (but sadly, depending on which design consultancy you are briefing, it sometimes doesn't, so you'd better say it anyway) that a new design should communicate the brand's proposition and should reflect and enhance its personality.

Beyond these two key objectives, you might want to define others in terms of perceived value (eg 'make it look like it costs 50p more'), or usage-suitability ('reflect the brand's strategic shift from breakfast to evening consumption'), or target market ('broaden its appeal from teenagers to young adults'). And you will probably want to include an objective related to shelf-impact, though this is in my view an over-rated virtue – there is no demonstrable correlation in any market between shelf impact and brand share – and is in any case something that will be achieved automatically if the principles of Total Branding are followed, by virtue of what will in consequence be a highly distinctive identity.

Whatever objectives are set, they should again be defined at the 'big picture' level, and expressed in terms of ends not means (so 'enhance the brand's appeal to young children' not 'incorporate cartoon imagery onto the pack'; 'improve brand recognition at point-of-sale' not 'increase the size of the logo').

Be ready, depending on which design consultancy you are talking to, to have these objectives challenged. There is always more than one way to skin a cat, and your design consultancy may well want to propose alternative design objectives which they feel would better help in the achievement of the overall marketing objectives. Or they may feel that a particular objective is unrealistic, or else is in conflict with other objectives. It is in ways such as this that a good design consultancy should be able to add value to your own thinking.

Indeed, depending on the nature of the design consultancy you are talking to, you might want to end the initial brief at this point, inviting them to investigate the rest of it themselves as part of the planning process. This might be the best way to approach certain kinds of NPD projects in particular, or projects for existing brands on which relatively little recent consumer research has been done.

In a pitch situation, ending the initial brief at this point would be a good way of challenging the candidates on your pitch-list to think through the issues. This way you will (a) learn a great deal about their strategic capabilities and approach, and (b) open the door to have value added to your own thinking.

Otherwise, an ideal client brief would go on as follows:

The Target Market

The target market should be defined at two levels: the broad and the narrow. At the broad level, you need to describe the characteristics which the broad mass of your brand's target consumers have in common. (For example, 'Working mums with kids are in this market primarily for convenience as they are time-poor and pragmatic in their attitudes towards this particular product field. It is a field in which they allow their kids a fairly high degree of influence over brand choice.')

At the narrow level (and this is the difficult bit for the average brand manager who yearns to define his target market as 'everyone'!) it helps to paint a word-picture of the absolutely core target consumer *as an individual*. So she is not 25–45, she is 35. She is not 'biased towards the South of England', she lives in Guildford. She is not only working, but more specifically she works as a claims manager in an insurance company. And so on.

All of this might sound ridiculous, and of course in a way it is. But whereas the phrase 'BCI working women aged 25–45 and biased towards the South of England' is meaningless to the average designer (and therefore of little or no help in guiding his or her creativity) the description of a particular individual makes the target market human. It creates, in the designer's mind, a striking picture of the person for whom he or she is designing, which makes it much more likely that appropriate design work will result.

The theory here, of course, is that if the core consumer has been accurately described, and if a piece of brand design is effective in communicating with that core consumer, then it won't be far wrong for the rest of the target market either.

One final word on this subject, and here I am indebted to Steve Henry, one of the creative partners in the ad agency Howell Henry Chaldecott Lury. Steve once told me that he finds it important that the description of the core consumer is written in such a way that he feels he *likes* that person. I'm ashamed to admit that this had never really occurred to me before, but it makes obvious sense.

So much creative work today, both in advertising and in pack design, is actually quite patronizing towards its target consumers, either shouting at them or treating them as idiots.

This tendency may well stem, at least in part, from briefs which define the target market in dismissive or patronizing terms. We all communicate more respectfully, and more effectively, with people we like. I think that's what David Ogilvy meant when he once wrote: 'the consumer is not a moron, she's your wife.'

The Competitive Environment

The first step in describing the brand's competitive environment is to define the 'frame of reference' in which it operates. As discussed in more detail in Chapter 3, careful thought needs to be given to this, because the frame of reference may vary depending on whether one's perspective is product-based, retail-based or consumer-based. Usually the consumer-based perspective will be the most useful.

Having defined the frame of reference, the next step is to list the specific brands which most commonly appear on the same consumer repertoire as our own, together with a brief analysis of how each is positioned.

Finally you might tell your design consultancy (though a good one would do its own analysis of this anyway) which competitive brands are most frequently merchandised directly alongside your brand on shelf. The point of this is that a good designer should be able to 'use' the adjacent brands to throw yours forward visually (a much more effective approach to getting shelf-impact than the more common method of using strident graphics and overblown logos).

Brand Proposition and Brand Personality

As the whole argument of this book is that good packaging design is above all else about communicating the brand's proposition, in a way which brings to life its personality, this part of the brief is pretty crucial.

We've already discussed propositions and brand personalities in some detail in earlier chapters, but two points are worth reiterating here.

The proposition must be single-minded. (There is a no-doubt apocryphal story of a creative director demonstrating the error of his ways to a client who wanted four distinct propositions in one, by throwing four sugar lumps across the table at him whilst shouting 'catch'. Needless to say, the client missed them all, but when a single sugar lump was thrown he caught it with ease.) And it should be expressed in words which are simple, concrete and positive. A good proposition should be richly evocative of visual metaphors, literally inspiring the designers to come up with a big visual idea. So, for example, 'the most delicious mix of exotic taste sensations' is a less inspiring proposition than 'a carnival in a can'.

So far as the brand personality is concerned, I would stress again the importance of distinguishing the *brand's* personality from that of its target consumers. They may sometimes be one and the same, but very often they are not. The test is, if the brand itself were literally to come to life as a human being, what kind of person would it be?

Mandatories and Executional Guidelines

Under 'mandatories' you should detail only those things that are truly mandatory – the corporate logo which, because it appears on 64 other brands, is not going to be changed just because a different one might look better on this particular brand; the legally obligatory product descriptor and any rules governing its use; rules governing the treatment or positioning of contents information, eco symbols, bar codes and the like.

'Executional guidelines' is the part of the brief where you might discuss your own views on category equities, brand equities, strengths and weaknesses of the current design, etc. But needless to say, the strength with which such views are expressed should correlate to some extent with the amount of consumer research evidence which supports them.

Production Constraints and Guidelines

This heading is fairly self-explanatory. Be careful here not to be over-restrictive or directional. Production management has not traditionally been a strong point of many design consultancies, and you need to judge the capabilities of the people you are talking to with care, but a good design production manager can often, working in tandem with your own production people, find opportunities for improvement in areas that seemed at first glance to offer only constraints.

Aspects to consider here include materials, shapes, filling-line considerations, print processes, number of colours, environmental issues, tamper-evidence and safety considerations, as well as specifying the format in which final artwork is required.

Contacts, Timings and Budgets

Finally, it is helpful to provide (and given the importance of teamwork discussed earlier, I am surprised at how seldom the initial brief does provide) the names and telephone numbers of key people your design consultancy will want to confer with. This list should include:

- your packaging production manager;

- your trade marketing manager;

- the account director at your ad agency, PR agency, sales promotion consultancy and direct marketing agency as relevant.

Ideal timing for the project should be included, but don't impose false deadlines. This is the embodiment of your brand we're dealing with here, and right is better than quick (though sometimes it will be necessary to be both right *and* quick).

So far as budgets are concerned, you might (especially in a pitch situation) want the design consultancy to propose what they judge will be required. But if you do have a fixed budget, and it cannot in any circumstances be exceeded, you will save a lot of time and trouble for all concerned if you state this in the initial brief.

DRAWING UP A SHORTLIST TO PITCH

Let's suppose that, instead of briefing one firm, you have decided to call a pitch for the project. The first step is to decide what kind of design consultancy is appropriate for the task in hand. This isn't to say that your pitch list should include only a narrowly defined 'type' of firm, but to get on your list they should all meet certain key criteria at least, having in common certain characteristics which you know are going to be critical when it comes to the final decision. This should really go without saying, but on more than one occasion my own company has put a lot of thought and effort into a pitch, only to be told at the end that we haven't won the business because of some factor which the client knew about right at the outset (or could easily have found out). There can be few more frustrating experiences in business than working long evenings and weekends on a pitch document only to find that the content of that document is (and always was) completely irrelevant because 'you are too small, and we want a bigger agency' or vice versa, or because 'you're based in London and we've decided we need a more local consultancy', or because 'you've had no direct experience in our particular marketplace'. Rejected on such grounds, it's hard to choke back the anguished response: 'But you knew that from the beginning!'

Sometimes, to be fair, factors which turn out to be decisive only emerge during the pitch process itself. You may not know that you want a larger agency until, having invited a small one to pitch, you find you can never get hold of anybody apart from the junior designer and the receptionist because there are only three senior people and they are always out at meetings.

Nevertheless, it should usually be possible to define in advance at least two or three key attributes which you already know will be vital. Dimensions might include:

- size;

- location;

- experience of international projects;

- NPD experience;

- strategic planning capabilities;

- digital artwork facilities.

All the above (and there are doubtless a few others) are easily ascertainable matters of fact, and having decided which facts

107

matter, you should be ruthless in eliminating from your potential pitch list any consultancy which fails to match your requirements. That way you will save everybody, including yourself, a good deal of time.

So, having decided upon a few key criteria, how do you go about drawing up your list of candidate design fims? Your initial search will probably use a combination of the following sources.

Personal Experience

The first source is consultancies you are currently working with, or have worked with in the past. In the case of an incumbent, if you are happy with their work, and with the relationship, do you really need to call a pitch at all? Why not simply award them the project? 'Because I want to see how other firms might approach it' is of course a fair answer, but be aware that the tendency to promiscuity (which seems to be more marked in respect of packaging design than it is for most other marketing services) is one of the reasons why you might feel a lesser depth of commitment from your design company than you do from your ad agency, for example. Appointed on an ad hoc project-by-project basis, and constantly having to pitch for every new project, even when it's for a long-standing client, design consultancies can be forgiven for feeling a little insecure, for pitching – given half a chance – to your direct competitors, for trying to maximize fee-income on every project with you, in case it turns out to be their last.

There are too many 'pitches for the sake of pitches' in design. Give your incumbent design firm the security of knowing that your business is theirs until and unless they screw it up, and you might be surprised at the level of commitment you receive in return. Certainly my personal experience is that a project which is awarded to Wickens Tutt Southgate *without* a pitch is seen as the kind of vote of confidence which absolutely demands – and therefore gets – our very best. When somebody shows real faith in you, you make extra efforts not to let them down.

On the other hand, of course, you may well have decided that – for whatever reason – your current design consultancy is probably not right for this particular project.

If so, don't think it a kindness to include them on the pitch list anyway. If they have no realistic chance of winning, put them out of their misery straight away, and be honest by telling them why.

Colleagues' Recommendations

The next most common source of inspiration in putting together a shortlist, after personal experience, is the recommendation of colleagues. The main thing to be wary of here is that nobody likes to be thought either ignorant or unhelpful, so everybody you ask will be able to recommend at least one design consultancy. But in many cases this recommendation will be based on fairly limited experience. Moreover, unless you've been explicit about what you are looking for, such recommendations may be based on quite different criteria from your own.

Forgive me if these points seem rather obvious. I make them, though, in the light of my own experience of frequently being asked by clients and agency mates if I 'know of a good' direct marketing outfit/PR consultancy/whatever, usually without being given any accompanying sense of what the questioner means by 'good'.

Direct Mail/Brochures etc

Marketeers are these days inundated with promotional materials from packaging design consultancies, and it is not surprising that many adopt the old 'bin the lot' technique for dealing with this stuff.

However, keeping abreast of what is available in the various marketing service specialisms is arguably a key element in a marketeer's job – and one which is increasing in importance as the marketing mix becomes more complex. On this basis, many of the more astute marketeers don't automatically bin every mailer or brochure that comes their way, but sift out those that seem to be different, or of potential future interest, building up a mini reference library for use in drawing up shortlists.

The most canny among them will periodically supplement

this library with their own 'finds' – a piece of work that is particularly admired, an article from the trade press, a list of Design Effectiveness Award winners – so that a good deal of information on the design consultancy marketplace is available when needed.

Independent Sources

The UK design consultancies' trade association, the Design Business Association (DBA), publishes an annual book of its members, listing their particular specialisms in each case, and a couple of paragraphs on their histories/philosophies/experience, etc. And at the time of writing, I believe something similar is planned on a pan-European scale by the Packaging Design Association of Europe (PDA Europe). In addition, the weekly magazine of the design industry, *Design Week*, publishes an annual 'book' of packaging designers which shows their work and can be another useful source.

Meanwhile, a specialist 'consultancy on consultancies' is available for clients wanting more in-depth, and more discreet, help in selecting design consultancies. The European Design Register is a growing business which acts as a source of expert impartial advice in matching client needs with agencies' abilities – either on an ad hoc basis or in helping clients put together, monitor and manage an ongoing roster of design firms.

Credentials Presentations

If any marketeer were to accept every offer from a design consultancy to 'show you our credentials', he or she would have no time for anything else.

But it may well be the case that, after working through the sources above, a large number of consultancies emerge as potential candidates for consideration. Rather than asking them *all* to pitch (ideally you want a shortlist of three for the pitch itself) it makes sense to draw up a 'long-list' from which credentials presentations will be invited in order to whittle them down to the final three.

You can learn a great deal about an agency from its credentials. Key things to consider include the following:

- Does the presentation communicate any kind of coherent theme or underlying philosophy? Or is it just a random selection of case histories?

- Does the consultancy appear to have a 'house style' in its creative work? If so, unless that house style happens to be a perfect match for your brand, you should eliminate them: the style of their work should reflect the needs of their clients' brands, not some particular design 'fashion' or company aesthetic.

- Where case histories are presented, does the consultancy talk convincingly about the marketing context and objectives for the project?

- And do they talk convincingly about results in the marketplace? Do you believe them? Things to watch out for here are vague hyperbolic statements such as 'sales went through the roof' or 'brand share doubled overnight'. Such phrases often mean 'we haven't got a clue what happened because by the time this work hit the market we'd long since moved on to other things and never bothered to ask this client how it was going'.

- Have they begun to think about your particular needs? Did they ask you any good questions (ideally before the meeting)? Do they seem to have tailored their presentation to make it as relevant as possible to you? When they present work from other markets, do they draw analogies with your own?

I am aware that in suggesting some of these criteria I run the risk of seeming to elevate presentation skills above design skills – and ultimately, of course, it is the latter you are interested in. But it seems to me that a consultancy which cannot talk intelligently about the business context in which its work has been developed, or which has not done at least a little homework on your own market, is not the sort of consultancy you can employ with any confidence.

There are designers who will say 'the work should speak for itself', but that is true only in an aesthetic sense, and you're not in the market for aesthetics alone. You are in the market for *applied creativity*, and you are entitled to be distrustful of a design consultancy which is less convincing on the 'applied' bit than it is on the 'creativity' bit.

This brings me on to perhaps the most crucial part of a credentials meeting: the questions you should ask them. Prospective clients in my experience tend to be too kind to design firms in credentials meetings. There is a tendency to sit politely through a presentation, perhaps asking a few routine questions about the agency's structure, staffing levels, etc, but generally to accept whatever agenda is set by the presentation itself.

Both parties would get more out of these meetings, it seems to me, if a more probing approach were taken.

In particular, you might (if you buy the general argument of this book so far) want to discriminate between those design consultancies which believe in *ideas*, and those which don't. So quiz them on the idea whenever they present a case history. What's the idea in this piece of work? What is it intended to communicate?

Quiz them, too, on the executional style in each case. If they answer in terms of the desired brand personality, and if they seem to have taken the competitive context into account, then they are probably worth proceeding with. If, on the other hand, they talk about executional style purely in terms of aesthetics, then beware – these people are Twinkies; if they can't get beyond shelf-impact in describing their work, then beware also – you're sitting with a bunch of Logo-louts.

Finally, why not pick two or three of their case histories at random, and ask for the name and telephone number of the principal client contact in each case? I have many times, in the past few years, volunteered such information to prospective clients, inviting them to take up references on us (and, I have to admit, this is always a calculated risk on my part – not all of our past clients have been wholly delighted with us!) but I have never been asked first.

This truly surprises me. If you were interviewing a candidate for a job, you would normally want to take up references from past employers. Why not do the same with a prospective design consultancy? You will probably learn more in a five-minute conversation with a recent client of theirs than you could in a whole fortnight of conversations with the person who is giving you the credentials presentation.

If you follow this process, you may well find that a pitch as such is unnecessary. On the basis of their credentials, their answers to your questions about their work, and what their clients say about them, you may find that a clear winner emerges from your 'long-list'. If so, why not move straight to a discussion of timings and budgets and (assuming you can agree on these) appoint them?

If not, you should at least be in a position by now to draw up a shortlist of three for a pitch.

HOW NOT TO RUN A PITCH

Never, never ask design consultancies to do speculative creative work in a pitch situation.

Why not? Well, for a start, unless you disagree with every word in this book so far, it should be obvious that achieving Total Branding is not a superficial process, whereas a speculative creative pitch is exactly that.

Merely to understand and interpret the client's brief (to say nothing of the possible improvements to it that the planning process – as we shall see in the next chapter – can make) takes a considerable amount of time and thought, as does turning the brief into a big idea, as does executing it properly.

Common sense should tell you that no design consultancy (at least, not one that will still be in business by the time you get to the final artwork stage) can afford to do everything it takes to do the job properly for free, with no guarantee of earning anything at all on the project let alone recovering the upfront investment.

So what you will get in a speculative creative pitch is a whole bunch of superficial 'concepts', knocked out by whichever designers happened to have a bit of time on their hands. There is an outside chance that the perfect solution will be among them. But it is about as likely as the next Pope being a Muslim.

'Ah, but', you may say, 'we don't expect to see the perfect solution, we just want to get an idea of the way the candidate consultancies work, and of their creative standards.' To which I would say that good design consultancies don't work this way at all, or if they do, in a moment of desperation, agree to take part in such an exercise, you will learn how they work when they have taken temporary leave of their professionalism, not how they work normally. As for learning about their creative standards, is taking stabs in the dark really 'creative'? Surely not in any useful sense of the word.

There are other reasons for not calling for speculative creative work:

- Any consultancy doing it is either dreadfully overstaffed (in which case they may be about to go bust) or 'stealing' time off the projects of fee-paying clients (in which case they will surely do the same to you if you become a fee-paying client).

- In the UK, the practice is banned under the Code of Conduct of the DBA, the design consultancies' trade association, and as most of the best consultancies are members of the DBA, you won't be able to get them on your pitch list.

- It starts what needs to be a positive and trusting working relationship off on the wrong foot, and relationships which start on the wrong foot seldom recover.

- Either you are not getting the consultancy's best work (in which case why bother?) or they are giving away their best work for free (in which case they are obviously low on self-respect). How can you respect a design consultancy which does not respect itself?

- You should have been able to satisfy yourself about their creative abilities from seeing their credentials.

And then there's perhaps the best reason of all:

- There's a better way of running a pitch.

HOW TO RUN A PITCH

If superficial speculative creative work is not the answer, what is? The precise answer will vary from client to client, and from project to project, but in general terms what you should be looking for in a pitch is evidence of the candidate design consultancies having:

- understood your marketplace;
- understood your brand;
- understood your objectives;

114

■ thought about your brief in terms of the specific design issues it raises;

■ developed a programme which offers an intelligent, thorough, and efficient route to resolving all issues and fulfilling your objectives.

Beyond these basic criteria, you may well want to see evidence that the candidate consultancies can add value to your own thinking.

Going back to 'the ideal client brief' earlier in this chapter, you may have chosen to include in the initial brief only those sections up to and including 'design objectives'. Ending the initial brief there will often be a good idea if there are still questions in your own mind regarding the precise definitions of target market, brand proposition, brand personality, visual equities, etc.

Even if (as is more likely) these issues are pretty clear in your own mind, it may still be a good idea to leave them out of the initial brief, as you will thereby learn a great deal more about the thinking and approach of each of your candidate agencies:

■ Do they address themselves to these issues at all? If not, you might ask yourself how they got on your shortlist in the first place. A design consultancy which doesn't even think about such issues is not one which thinks about design as a communication tool. Certainly, it's not one from which you'll get Total Branding, or anything like it.

■ If they *have* addressed themselves to these issues, how have they done so? By asking you questions (fair enough) or by making sweeping assumptions or bold guesses to fill in the gaps (not fair enough)? By recommending a sensible programme of research to explore these issues (good) or by recommending answers based on their own, dipstick, 'asking-a-few-people-in-our-studio' type of research (not so good)?

■ Is there anything fresh or innovative in their approach to such issues? Might they be capable of offering new insights, or supplementing your own thinking about the brand in some way?

■ Have they thought about the role of packaging design in the context of the rest of the marketing mix?

By briefing your candidate consultancies only up to the definition of design objectives, and leaving them to think through the issues from there, you will have made them share with you the ways in which they *think* about packaging design, not just their routine processes and proposed fees.

You will have thus given yourself some powerful tools with which to distinguish one consultancy from another. And you will have opened up your own mind to the possibility of an approach which is different from, and conceivably better than, the one you had in mind originally.

Now let's suppose you have chosen to give the full brief, executional guidelines and all, to your pitch candidates.

In these circumstances, what you are looking for is, above all, evidence that they have understood it. But even here, you should be ready to have aspects of your brief probed and challenged. The brief that cannot be improved by being looked at from a different perspective probably doesn't exist. So expect new issues to be raised.

Finally, there is the question of how they approach the pitch itself. Have they treated it as a dialogue, keeping in touch between briefing and pitch presentation? Or did it all go quiet until the day of the pitch itself? There is a delicate balance to be struck here. You don't want to be pestered by your candidate agencies every five minutes, nor do you want to feel that you are having to spoon-feed them. So they should be doing quite a bit of their pitch-work on their own. On the other hand, the occasional call to seek clarification of some aspect of your brief, or to solicit more information, or indeed to get your input into their own emerging thinking, may well increase your confidence that you could have a good working relationship with these people – or not, as the case may be!

Of course, after all this, you might still be tempted by an outfit which offers a superficial, speculative creative solution. Or, even worse, to pick the winner on price alone. But if so, you have only yourself to blame if you end up with ineffective packaging design as a result.

HOW TO CHOOSE A NEW DESIGN CONSULTANCY: A CHECKLIST

Stage 1: Preparation

- What are your key criteria?
- What type of consultancy are you therefore looking for?

Stage 2: The initial trawl

- Colleagues' recommendation?
- Relevant direct mail received, or ads seen?
- DBA annual, and *Design Week* book?
- Other brands whose design you admire?
- Help from European Design Register, or other consultants?

Stage 3: Credentials

- Coherent philosophy or approach?
- 'House-style', or brand-specific work?
- Where are the *ideas*?
- Marketing context? Results?
- Recent client references?

Stage 4: Briefing the shortlist

- End with objectives, or give full brief?
- What kind of questions do they ask?

Stage 5: The pitch

- Dialogue or monologue?
- How do they think about what they do?
- Understanding of your brief?
- Issues raised? Fresh thinking?
- New insights? Value added to your own thinking?
- Sensible process and programme?
- Chemistry?

7

HOW IT'S DONE

THE ROLE OF DESIGN PLANNING

Total Branding, as we have seen, is about a comprehensive, 'whole pack', approach to branding; it is about using every aspect of a brand's packaging design actively to communicate that brand's proposition and personality, via a big idea and an appropriate style of execution.

The phrase 'Total Branding' therefore describes a particular approach to the creative task of packaging design – *but one which is rooted firmly in brand strategy.*

Indeed, its very potency in this regard makes it potentially quite dangerous, in the sense that weaknesses or flaws in the underlying strategy will be more evident in a pack designed according to the Total Branding philosophy than they would be in one which isn't.

After all, if Total Branding brings a brand's proposition to life at point-of-sale (as it does) then it can just as easily bring to life a poor proposition as a good one. If it brings to life the brand's personality (as it does), then it can just as easily give expression to a personality which alienates a brand's target consumers as to one which attracts them.

So, if the whole exercise is to be worthwhile, it's pretty important that both the brand's proposition, and its personality, are correctly defined in the first place, ie:

- true to the brand;

- relevant and credible in the context of its product fields;

- motivating to its target consumers;

- distinctive in the competitive context.

Design planning starts with this – with the necessity of making sure we are not building on sand, by making sure that the fundamentals of proposition and personality are suitably robust.

It goes on to test every other aspect of the brand's strategic infrastructure, at the same time making sure that a thorough and detailed understanding is built up of the contexts in which the new design will have to work.

Of course, much of this ground may already have been covered in the client's initial brief. And certainly there will, depending on the nature of that brief, be areas which do not need to be re-examined in any depth. There is, as the cliché says, no point in reinventing the wheel, and most briefs will already contain a good wheel or two. But even those, if you'll forgive the slightly desperate attempt to turn a cliché into a metaphor, might benefit from a better set of tyres!

We'll look in more detail in a moment at some of the specific ways in which (and tools with which) planning can add value to a brief.

First, I'd like to dwell for a minute on the ultimate purpose of it, in the context of packaging design. The purpose of planning might be expressed as 'avoiding what's wrong and inspiring what's right'.

So it's a dual role, and the first part of that duality is more straightforward than the second. The avoidance of wrong is largely a question of thoroughness. Providing the design task has been fully considered from every angle, using appropriate research and sensible analysis, it should usually be possible to avoid major cock-ups (disasters such as the Wall's sausages episode, described back in Chapter 3, are thankfully rare). Actively to inspire what's right for the brand, however, is a more difficult feat.

It demands insight in analysis, and incisiveness in interpretation. It demands that, of all the many things that the designer will have to bear in mind in developing the ultimate solution, the one key thought that lies at the heart of it is correctly identified and inspirationally expressed. Its expression may be a phrase, a single word, an analogy or even an image. However it is expressed, that one key thought should be the catalyst which sparks the imagination of the designers, thereby helping to inspire the great creative solution rather than the merely good one.

Probably the most difficult thing a planner has to do is to find that one, key, inspirational thought (and, if I may be permitted a personal note at this point, here seems as good a place as any to apologize to all the designers down the years whom I have personally failed in this regard, burdening them with pages of worthy stuff to help them 'avoid what's wrong' but too often providing only a damp squib where the inspirational firecracker should have been).

The next most difficult thing is to strike the right balance, in briefing, between the two parts of the paradox: between the worthy and the inspiring, the thorough and the incisive, the constraining and the liberating.

Leonardo da Vinci perhaps had only one part of this paradox in mind when he wrote that 'art is born of constraint, and dies of liberty', whereas, to my mind, the paradox was perfectly captured by John Webster, the great advertising creative, when he asked his planners to 'give me the freedom of a tight brief'.

The key to resolving this paradox lies, I believe, in thinking about the creative brief as a *process* rather than as a piece of paper – and we'll come on to this shortly.

But first, let's turn to some specific aspects of the overall brief, and to some of the ways in which planning may make a contribution in working towards Total Branding.

BUYERS AND USERS: STRIKING THE RIGHT BALANCE

For many brands, the buyer is not the same person as the ultimate user. Both are important, as in most cases either one might be responsible for choosing which brand is bought, and either one might have power of veto.

Where this is the case (brands bought by mum for consumption by her kids is the obvious situation, but women buying for their men or vice versa can be even more difficult) descriptions of both will usually feature in the brief. The tricky thing is to define the right balance in communication terms for packaging design to strike.

On this issue, advertising has much the easier task. It is perfectly possible to develop advertising aimed entirely at the buyer, for example, or entirely at the user, and via careful media scheduling to avoid talking to the one in language intended for the other. It is perfectly possible, indeed, to develop two campaigns – one for each audience – to run in parallel with one another.

For the most part, packaging design cannot be approached in this way. The same pack will be seen by and handled by – and therefore has to communicate with – both buyer and user.

Even in those cases where it *is* possible to split the communication (the multipack which talks primarily to mum on the supermarket shelf, but which contains individual packs which talk more directly to her kids when she breaks open the multipack at home) there is every likelihood that both audiences will see both messages, causing potential confusion or dilution of brand image.

So careful thought needs to be given to the exact role of packaging design, for both buyer and user, at each stage of the brand's journey from retail display onwards. Which are the critical stages for each person? Can their different needs be interpreted in such a way that they become complementary rather than conflicting for the designer to deal with?

Sometimes, these issues will need to be explored in qualitative research as part of the planning phase prior to design work starting.

Often, the answer will lie in designing primarily for the end-user, but overlaying a few executional guidelines which reflect what the buyer *thinks* the user will find appealing. Notoriously, for example, adults' perceptions of what kids will find motivating tend to be somewhat off the mark (even when it's their own kids they are talking about) so the designers will need to be briefed to 'aim off' accordingly.

OBSERVATION AT POINT-OF-SALE

It is important, for two reasons, that time is spent at point-of-sale before the final creative brief is put together.

First of all, the designers will need to be armed with a good understanding of the merchandising context in which our brand will find itself:

■ How is this product field merchandised overall? What kind of fixture units are most commonly used?

■ What are lighting conditions like?

■ Does our brand tend to be merchandised at eye level, higher or lower?

■ What's the immediate 'brandscape' of competitive brands surrounding our own? What are the most common immediate adjacencies?

■ How many facings do we typically get in the most important store-type?

■ Is any part of the pack routinely obscured, for example by a shelf-strip or overhang?

■ Is this product field well-merchandised in terms of the main face of each pack being displayed? Or is there a regular danger of a 'secondary' face (top or sides) being faced forward?

■ How orderly, or how chaotic, is the overall visual impression of this sector?

All of these factors will or should have a bearing on the ultimate design, so it helps if they have been noted and incorporated into the creative brief.

A design consultancy that spends lots of time in-store will probably have a friendly store manager or two in each retail sector, in which case they will probably be allowed to take photographs of the relevant fixtures for the designer's future reference.

Of course, most designers will want to see the environment for themselves at some point anyway but a permanent record of it back in the studio is usually useful if only as an *aide-mémoire*.

The second reason it's important for the planner to spend some time in-store is to watch the customers. In product fields where traffic is light, this can be a time-consuming exercise, but one that is nearly always worthwhile. When I say 'watch the customers' I don't mean just to see who they are (though this can indeed be useful, either to put flesh on the bones of the target market definition in the client's brief, or occasionally to sow seeds of doubt as to whether that definition was accurate to begin with). I mean, in addition, to see what they do.

You can learn a terrific amount of relevant and useful stuff just from watching how people shop in a particular category.

- Do they devote browsing time to this category, or is it a case of grab and go?

- Where coding systems are being employed (eg to differentiate between flavours, or sizes, or strengths, or types) do they seem to be working or are they simply missed by the consumer?

- Which elements of the 'design language' in this market place seem to be the critical ones used by consumers in making brand choices?

- Supplementing the work described earlier regarding buyers and users, if (for example) this is a market featuring mum buying for kids, how much say do the kids seem to get when they are accompanying mum round the shop?

- Overall, does this product field seem to represent an 'easy buy' for consumers, or do they look like they are finding it confusing or difficult?

The value of this kind of observation, and these kinds of questions, was brought home to me in the planning phase of our first work for Tomy. Briefed to redesign their pre-school toy packs, it was through close observation at point-of-sale that we first realized the enormous confusion that was being caused by toy manufacturers' (and retailers') tendency to lump all pre-school toys together.

In fact – as we subsequently confirmed in follow-up qualitative discussion groups – there is an enormous difference in consumers' minds between the values they are looking for when buying for an infant, and those they are seeking when buying for a toddler. There are other differences within each life-stage, but the moment at which an infant gets up and starts toddling about marks an absolute sea-change in parents' requirements from toys.

Prior to the child toddling, the key dimensions are safety, charm and faculty development. Once toddling has begun, different key dimensions come to the fore, namely activity, fun, durability and learning.

It was on the basis of this work that we were able to recommend to Tomy that their pre-school toys (hitherto packaged, like most of their competitors', in one fairly monolithic style) should be segmented into two quite distinct ranges – First Fun for infants, Big Fun for toddlers – each with a very different identity.

The two resulting ranges are each examples of Total Branding, whereby the whole pack is used to communicate brand values, but because of this new segmentation there are now, in effect, two brands. Each has a much sharper proposition, and a much more relevant and motivating personality, as a consequence. And, just as importantly, the consumer can now easily tell them apart at point-of-sale.

(Following this work, Tomy overtook Fisher-Price to become, for the first time, pre-school market leader in the UK. A year later, Tomy and Wickens Tutt Southgate won a Design Effectiveness Award for it.)

BRAND FAMILIES

The Tomy example described above illustrates an increasingly common difficulty for the purveyor of Total Branding. At what level do we define 'the brand'? For whilst there are still thousands of stand-alone brands offering tightly focused product ranges, there are thousands more (and their numbers are growing) which have a rather more complex branding structure.

So far in this book, I have tended – for simplicity and clarity – to use examples primarily of the stand-alone type of brand. But it's time now to look at the more complex type, which can involve a two-tier, three-tier or even (as can happen in the case of a retail brand, for example) a four-tier structure.

The top tier is typically the 'corporate brand' (Tomy, Cadbury's, McVities, Heinz, etc), whilst the lowest tier is usually described as the 'sub-brand'. The brand – in the sense in which we have been using the word in this book – usually sits in the middle tier, though in the case of retailers or large corporations there may be a 'divisional brand' or a 'range brand' between it and the top, corporate level.

How does Total Branding deal with this complexity? In theory (and if the entire brand structure were being designed simultaneously) the answer is: totally!

If there is any logic to the overall brand architecture, then a sub-brand's proposition is a sub-set of (and is embraced within) the proposition of the brand of which it is a part, which in turn is but a sub-set of (and again, is embraced within) the overall proposition of the corporate brand.

Theoretically, therefore, Total Branding can be achieved on all three levels via an idea within an idea within an idea. A strong idea can be just as multilayered as the brand structure which spawns it.

In the same way, so far as brand personality is concerned, there is no theoretical difficulty in conceptualizing a brand family (father–son–little sister, for example) in which each member has his or her own particular traits of character, whilst all share common family characteristics to the extent that they are clearly all part of the same family.

So much for the theory. In practice, however, it is extremely rare for an entire brand family to be created simultaneously, so the reality tends to fall some way short of the theory.

Parts of the brand family are likely to have well-established identities, so the Total Branding approach needs to be modified to reflect reality. On the top level, for example, very few corporate brands have a tightly focused consumer proposition, so it is hardly surprising that very few are represented in design terms by anything you could call an idea. Most are represented merely by a logo. In recent years, Cadbury's has probably come closest to turning its logo into an idea. In its advertising, the corner of the screen or page is torn back, as though ripping open a chocolate bar, to reveal the Cadbury's signature stamped into chocolate. But this idea has not been totally carried through on the packaging of its brands.

The fact that most corporate brands have only a logo to represent them is not necessarily a problem, though, so long as it is acknowledged that such entities are brands only in the blandest sense of the word. Indeed, I would suggest a 'Total

Branding test' as a potentially useful contribution to board room debates about the wisdom or otherwise of pushing the corporate brand instead of trying to support a number of individual brands. The test is, does the corporate brand have a sufficiently focused and single-minded proposition that one could imagine it being encapsulated in a single visual idea? If so, throwing all the company's weight behind the corporate brand might very well make sense, for it clearly qualifies as a meaningful brand. If not, then such a move would probably be a mistake. If a strong yet unifying design idea cannot be envisaged, then you haven't got a strong and unifying proposition. Which in turn means you haven't really got a *brand* in the pure sense, just a name.

The same test in reverse applies to the lower-level brand/sub-brand relationship. Is the core idea which expresses the brand's proposition capable (perhaps with a slight twist if necessary) of embracing the sub-brand also? If so, fine. If not – if to communicate its particular proposition the sub-brand needs an idea all of its own, quite distinct from that of the brand – then the chances are you haven't got a sub-brand at all. You've got a parasite, a leech which is busy diluting your brand's meaning. You've fallen into Ries and Trout's 'free ride trap'.

If the potential for interlocking visual ideas is the test of a robust brand structure, it has to be said that establishing kinship via related personality attributes (and, therefore, related executional styles) is somewhat easier to achieve. And in practice, this is how such brand families are usually linked.

The reason for raising this whole issue at this point in the design process is twofold. Firstly, I'd like to suggest that slapping a parental logo in the top left-hand corner is not the only way – or even necessarily the best way – to link the different levels of the brand family structure, and secondly to say that now, after the design objectives have been agreed, but before creative work starts, is the time to think this issue through.

As with the other issues in this section, guidance from qualitative research may be helpful in understanding where parameters lie.

THE HIERARCHY OF INFORMATION

In order of importance, first comes the idea (to express the brand's proposition), closely followed by how it's executed (to express the brand's personality). But what next? Product support? Variant type? Secondary benefit? Definition of usage role? Definition of main intended user? Communication of specific taste, or size, or ingredients? Price? Ecological or environmental facts? Corporate parentage? Usage instructions?

Packaging design, irrespective of whether or not it aspires to Total Branding, will have to deal, in its final physical and graphic resolution, with any or all of the above, and potentially with other communication points besides.

The question is, in what order of priority? Several different points are likely to be important – perhaps even 'equally important'. But I would suggest that design cannot – or, at least, should not try to – communicate two or more things with equal prominence. If a pack design is to work as a properly balanced whole, there needs to be a clear hierarchy of importance, and this not only in terms of *what* is communicated, but also in terms of *how*.

In considering how to carry off any one piece of communication, and how to separate it from other pieces, designers have a number of different variables to play with: size, position on pack, colour, typography, graphics (perhaps a series of minor variations on the core idea? perhaps a subsidiary idea, separate from the main one?), the amount of space in which this particular piece of communication is allowed to sit, physical pack shape, materials, photographic style (and/or illustrative style, as the case may be), and finally – if words are to play a part in this particular piece of communication – there is the choice of which words and how many.

A complex packaging range, in terms of its complete communication needs, may well feature the conscious deployment of most if not all of the tools listed above.

As a purely hypothetical example, a hosiery brand, comprising a wide range of products segmented on a wide range of variables, might result in design tools being aligned with communication needs as shown in Table 7.1.

Table 7.1 *Hypothetical alignment of design tools and communication needs*

Variable design tool	Communication need
Overall unifying idea	Communicate overall brand proposition.
Overall style of execution	Convey overall brand personality.
Variations on core idea	Identify and differentiate principal sub-ranges.
Pack shapes	Match individual products to broad price bands (eg everyday/luxury).
Pack materials/textures	Communicate product-specific benefit of finished effect (eg sheer, glossy, opaque).
Position of typography	Consistent treatment of item-specific information such as size, colour, denier.
Size and/or use of space	Isolate, within the above, denier (for example) as the most important.
Colour	Discriminate between distinct product types (eg tights v. stockings v. pop-sox).
Photographic style	Suggest usage occasion for different ranges within, or perhaps cutting across, these product types.
Words	Secondary product support and contents information (eg % lycra content).

The question of which tool to use for which communication task is ultimately for the designers to work out – resolving such complexities is, after all, a key skill in the designer's craft.

Where the planner needs to help is in determining (together with the client, and often – again – via the sensitive use of qualitative consumer research) what exactly those communication tasks are, and *in what order of priority*. After all, it is no good using a range of different vehicles to satisfy a range of different information needs if, at the end of the day, they are all used with equal weight and prominence. The end result will still be a confusing range of packs, and a confused consumer.

A clear hierarchy is required, based on a thorough understanding of the consumer's 'decision-tree' in that particular market.

RESEARCHING EQUITIES

Back in Chapter 3, we looked at category equities (those features of 'design language' which are common to a market category, and which can be helpful or even necessary to consumers in classifying a brand as belonging to that particular category or 'frame of reference') and brand equities (those features of a particular brand's design by which it is known and loved by its consumers).

One of the points I made earlier is that it can be extremely difficult, in both cases, to discriminate between meaningful equities and meaningless clutter; or, in the standard cliché in this area, between baby and bathwater (as in the desire to avoid chucking out the one with the other).

There are several issues, as we have discussed, on which fresh qualitative research might helpfully shed light during the design planning process, but perhaps none more so than this one.

If you don't *know* which aspects of a category's 'design language' are critical in giving your brand the right frame of reference, and/or if you don't *know* what your brand's true visual equities are, in terms of both saliency and contribution, then it seems to me you are running an unnecessarily high risk of failure in any pack design project.

In the case of an NPD project leading to the creation of a new brand, category equities will be particularly important, whereas for an established brand undergoing relaunch or line extension, brand equities will probably be more critical.

In either case, it is the consumer's perspective (as opposed to the brand management team's, or the design consultancy's) that you should be interested in. And there are some straightforward qualitative consumer research techniques which can significantly reduce the risk of mistakes in these areas.

Most of the better packaging design consultancies can these

days contribute usefully (in terms of thinking, and preparing relevant stimulus materials) to such research. Some have developed their own research approaches and methodologies. At Wickens Tutt Southgate, we have a fairly comprehensive research programme called VIEW ('Visual Interrogation of Equity Worth'), which is sufficiently proprietary for me not to want to disclose full details here in the 'public domain' of this book, but if I describe some of the main underlying assumptions, and mention a few of the core tools and techniques, you will get the general idea.

Here, then, are some of the principal assumptions:

- An equity, to be worthy of the name, must be high in both saliency and contribution. In other words, not only must it enjoy a high degree of recognition amongst the target market, but it must also actively contribute to meaning or values. Equities, once spotted, should be treated with care.

- Beyond equities, there are signifiers and identifiers (high in saliency and able to signify membership of a particular category, or identify a particular brand, but low or lacking in active contribution beyond these basic levels).

- At the lowest level are the generics and the passengers: visual elements which may or may not be remembered but which signify nothing, identify nothing, contribute nothing; they are simply *there*, and might just as usefully not be.

- To return to equities, their current visual form may matter less than their *worth*, ie what they actively contribute to the consumer's understanding of the category or of the brand. Treating an equity with respect does not necessarily mean treating it as a fixed and sacrosanct design element. Once its worth has been properly understood, there may be better ways of communicating the same thing even more strongly. It may, in other words, be the equity's *worth* that you need to keep and build on, rather than the visual equity itself in its current form.

- Equities do not exist in isolation, but rather in relationship with other elements, and with the gestalt of the brand's identity, in a broader competitive context. So for many years, its role and worth will almost certainly

133

have changed – and will, indeed, be changing all the time as the context within which it is 'decoded' changes.

With these assumptions in mind, research techniques and tools to explore category and brand equities include:

- *Drawing from memory.* Arm consumers, in group discussions, with blank drawing pads and a wide range of coloured pens. Then, with no prior prompts from branded materials, get them to draw particular brands' packs from memory, going on to discuss with the whole group what each of them has drawn and why.

- *Cut-downs.* A range of modified pack designs, each with a different element missing. Used as stimuli in groups, these help identify not only the saliency or otherwise of potential equities, but also their contributions to meaning and values, via a discussion of how perceptions of the brand may have shifted as different elements have 'disappeared'.

- *Name-swapping.* Swap the logos and brand names on different pack designs from the same market, then discuss why (and if!) the resulting designs would be 'wrong' for the brands which they now proclaim themselves to be.

- *Sub-texts.* For each potential equity, have your design consultancy prepare visual image boards or collages which portray a range of different potential underlying meanings. It is important here to go beyond the obvious, but not to go so far as to prepare anything which would be incredible or implausible in the context of the brand.

The key point I want to make, via all of the above, is that so far as visual equities are concerned, it is both possible and – when it comes to writing the creative brief – rewarding, to go beyond the obvious issues of awareness, recognition and saliency, exploring the deeper issues of worth, meaning and contribution.

This way, fewer design 'babies' will be lost, and an awful lot more 'bathwater' can confidently be washed down the plughole.

THE CREATIVE BRIEF

The first thing to stress here is that there is a difference between the initial client brief, discussed in the previous chapter, and the final creative brief – and not just because the design planning process may have shed some extra light on a few issues in the meanwhile. An even more fundamental difference results from each having a different role, and a different audience.

The initial client brief has the primary roles of defining objectives, placing these in the right marketing context, and delineating the broad parameters of the project.

The final creative brief, by contrast, has a narrower focus on inspiring the most effective, Totally Branded, creative response.

The initial client brief is written for the whole design consultancy (or more than one, if it is used to start a pitch) and its audiences may also include the client's management, and sometimes other types of agency.

The final creative brief, again by contrast, is prepared with just one audience in mind: the designer(s) who will actually be working on the project.

There is no single 'right way', therefore, to write this brief. Different designers work in different ways; issues which one will need explaining in some detail, another will grasp from a sentence; some understand marketing jargon, others don't; some want to know everything in the brief right from the outset, other prefer to consider it in stages.

Irrespective of the intrinsic merits of a creative brief, if it doesn't get through to the designer(s) who have to respond to it, it's a bad brief. The converse, of course, is also true – a brief which inspires truly effective creative work is, by definition, a good brief.

What this boils down to is the vital importance, at this stage, of personal communication. This is why it is usually a good idea to leave the final creative briefing to your design consultancy, to be handled internally as it sees fit.

Very often, in any case, the concept of 'the brief' as a single, all-embracing, written document, is not the best way to think about it. Good creative briefing can often be in the form of a dialogue spread over a number of days, or even weeks.

There will be a written summary of key aspects somewhere

along the way. But much of the briefing may best be accomplished verbally, and almost always there will be visual materials involved as well – image boards, competitive packs, stuff ripped out of magazines, photos of the point-of-sale environment, etc.

So the *form* of the creative briefing will differ from the initial client brief – and needs to be approached in a more flexible way.

The *content*, too, is likely to be different. As a general rule, nothing should go into the final creative briefing which does not have a direct implication in some way for the creative work. Much of the background and marketing context from the initial client brief, for example, has by now outlived its usefulness. It was there to help the consultancy's planners and account handlers to get a fix on the brand, and to help them think about the role for design, and consequent design objectives, in a broader way. The designers themselves – unless they are unusually marketing-literate designers – do not need to know this stuff, and shouldn't have to wade through it.

What they *do* need brings us back to the paradox discussed at the beginning of this chapter: they need both less and more! Less, in the sense that the whole brief needs to be distilled down to that one, core, inspirational thought which will focus their minds on the very essence of what's needed; more, in the sense that the planning stage should have amplified a whole bunch of issues (to do with the consumer, the point-of-sale environment, the competition and the hierarchy of information, etc) which will, or should, have a direct bearing on the final design.

The crux of the problem in creative briefing is how to deal with this paradox: how to give both less and more.

The answer is likely to be found in approaching it from the designer's point of view, tailoring the creative briefing to reflect an understanding of how each individual designer works.

HOW DESIGNERS DO IT

Needless to say, there are as many different answers to the question 'how do designers do what they do?' as there are designers. And when it comes to the most creative part of what they do, that moment of inspiration when a truly original creative idea is born, there is probably no answer at all. That bit is pure mystery, and shrivels and dies under the spotlight of logical analysis.

So it is with a great deal of trepidation that I include a section on this subject at all. I do so, though, in the belief that it is possible to convey at least the beginnings of an understanding of how creative designers approach what they do, and in the hope that by doing so, it might help marketeers to a greater appreciation of the design process, perhaps a greater respect for the need for adequate time in which to do it, and ideally, therefore, a better understanding of why it is almost always a false economy to skimp on budgets for the creative phases of a design project.

To dwell on this last point for a moment, I am constantly surprised at the willingness of marketeers to spend more on researching and evaluating design concepts than they are prepared to spend on having a concept created in the first place. Budgets for multiple mock-ups for quantitative research will sail through 'on the nod', whilst every last penny spent on creative concepts is begrudged. The blame for this state of affairs must be laid, at least in part, at the doors of we in the design community who have failed down the years to explain and justify the value of creativity.

Perhaps we have been misguided in explaining design budgets in terms of 'hourly rates', making explicit the linkage between time and money. To be sure, that's what it comes down to at the end of the day – the biggest single cost on a design project is the cost of having creative people sitting at their drawing-boards, or at their Macs, or even staring at the ceiling or gazing out of the window, whilst wrestling with your design problem.

But although that is in truth where the money goes, making it explicit in budget breakdowns does seem to give rise to an almost irresistible temptation to cut costs by cutting back on time.

Many consultancies have chosen to address this dilemma by taking what amounts to a loss-leader approach to the creative work itself, underselling it in the hope of recouping the time-costs later on, in their charges for mock-ups and artwork. But surely it would be better if the value of design time was better appreciated in the first place.

So what do designers actually do? Let's start with a list of all the things they have to think about:

Things to communicate:

- the brand's proposition;
- the brand's personality;
- specific benefits of specific products or variants, appropriately differentiated;
- all necessary information, in the right order of priority in each case.

Who we're communicating with:

- the person we want to buy this brand;
- the person we want to use it;
- the circumstances in which it is bought, and used;
- the buyer's frame of mind when buying;
- the user's frame of mind when using.

The context:

- the environment at point-of-sale;
- what competitive brands look like;
- what the immediate brandscape looks like;
- the environment in which the brand, once bought, will be stored and used.

Guidelines and constraints:

- category equities;
- brand equities;
- mandatory symbols and copy;
- printing and production parameters.

Available tools:

- materials and finishes;
- shapes and structures;

- colour;
- type;
- calligraphy;
- photography;
- illustration;
- graphic devices;
- spatial relationships.

The list above is probably not comprehensive, but it will do for our purposes here. The point is that nobody can possibly think about all of those things all at once. And thinking about any one of them opens up possibilities, and avenues for exploration, which can merely compound the complexity of what is already an incredibly complex task.

In truth, from the moment a briefing starts to the moment the final proof is signed off, what goes on in a designer's mind, whether consciously or not, is a constant process of synthesis, of drawing all those strands together, weighing and judging the whole while, until the perfect solution is reached. That said, I've never met a designer who ever thinks the perfect solution *has* been reached. In the designer's mind, there is always room for improvement, the problem is never completely cracked. But the longer he or she has to think about it, to wrestle with it, and indeed to *play* with it, the better the solution will be.

Being a designer is a 24-hour a day job. Not only because of deadlines, but also because a designer is either constantly thinking about the brief or is constantly stocking up visual vocabulary – remembering a particular colour combination or remembering the shape sunlight makes as it passes through a glass of wine.

There are very few rules regarding how designers do it. Each one has a different working process but there are a few common traits.

There are basically two types of idea; the blinding flash of inspiration (very rare indeed – few designers ever have one of these in an entire career) and the 'germs' which need to be nurtured, protected and constantly tested and evolved until they become viable.

There are a multitude of ways in which they create these

'germs'. They rarely get to a solution in one leap. They jump from one idea to another, like stepping stones, until they arrive somewhere new. Some think in almost logical straight lines. Others jump about seemingly at random.

Some think in pictures, looking for a 'visual language' to borrow or re-interpret in order to communicate the proposition. For example, if the proposition is 'smooth' they look for the visual language of smooth, perhaps as exemplified by smooth surfaces (marble) or smooth colours (pale yellow) or smooth symbols (babies bottoms!).

Others think in progressions or lists of words or phrases, for example smooth to soft, soft to silky, silky to flowing, flowing to water and so on.

Some designers need to be *visually* stimulated to get their minds going – they look through books, the subject matter of which is unimportant as long as there are lots of different pictures to trigger visual stepping stones.

Some think with their hands, constantly drawing or cutting up images to see where they end up. Others stare into space or out of the window, letting their minds wander in and out of a problem. And some do indeed have their best ideas in the bath!

Most designers use a combination of some or all of these processes. Others have yet different ways of doing things.

There are no rules and there are probably as many different ways of creative thinking as there are designers. Many designers need time to 'empty their brains' of as many different ideas as possible before deciding which ones may well bear fruit. Others know early on exactly where they want to get to, it's just getting there that takes time. After about 30 years in the business, the great American designer Herb Lubalin once said that his best idea was usually the first thing he thought of, he just didn't realise it until he'd considered all the other options.

What a designer draws at an early stage is quite often only a rough approximation of his or her idea. It is simply a vehicle for explanation and further exploration. Once an idea is starting to take shape the designer takes on the role of a scientist – constantly testing it, as one would a hypothesis, to see if it stands up to scrutiny.

Having evolved the 'germ' into a fully fledged idea, the designers then put themselves in the mind of the consumer, asking 'Will he or she take out what I have put in?', in other words 'are they hearing what I'm saying or are they hearing something different?' And so on, to the next idea, until they arrive at something great.

Whatever the individual designer's working process, his or her first problem is where to start. If it is impossible to think about every aspect of a creative brief all at once, where does a designer begin?

This is why it's important that the brief includes, at its heart, a succinct summation of the essence of the task. It is likely that this summation will include, or be closely related to, the brand proposition, because, if Total Branding is the aim, the proposition is where the designer's work starts in earnest.

Bearing in mind the core summation of the overall task, the designer will spend the first few days wrestling with visual ideas to bring the brand's proposition to life. Layout pads will be filled with initial thoughts, none of which will necessarily look anything like a pack design at this stage.

Depending on the individual designer's way of working, there may be lots of words, rough scribbles, perhaps images torn out of magazines or photocopied from reference books. The idea's the thing, and execution is hardly considered at all at this stage.

The first internal reviews, three or four days in, will focus on whittling down what may be thirty or forty 'initial thoughts' to perhaps five or six that seem to be the most promising. The creative director's role is pivotal here, both in the whittling down, and in suggesting new avenues for exploration if there seem to be routes which have not yet been considered.

Towards the end of the second week there will be a full team internal review. By now, executional considerations will have started to come into the picture. Whilst continuing to think primarily about the big idea, the designer will have begun to focus on the brand's personality, and the executional style which that suggests.

In theory, any idea is capable of being executed in an almost infinite variety of ways. In practice, however, certain ideas lend themselves more readily to particular styles of execution than others, and certain styles of execution in turn favour some ideas over others.

So by now, the synthesis of idea and execution is starting to take place. Still the focus is first and foremost on ideas. But now, the great mass of sketches and scraps in the layout pad contains many roughs that bear at least some resemblance to the pack.

At the end of the second week there may well be an interim meeting, or 'tissue meeting', with the client team. No attempt will be made to turn this into a 'presentation'. It's a working meeting, in which the client team is invited to share the design team's thinking to date. The rough layout pad will be used as stimulus for this discussion, but much that is in it will need to be talked around to explain it.

By the third week, lots of initial ideas will have been abandoned as insufficiently fruitful; others will still be in contention, with increasing amounts of executional thinking being brought to bear on them.

Further internal reviews follow, culminating in the decision to focus on one or more ideas to be worked up for the concept presentation to the client team, which usually takes place some time in the fourth week.

All being well, the recommended idea goes forward into design development. Only now does the focus shift fully onto executional considerations.

All other aspects of the brief (buyer and user, competitive context, point-of-sale environment, hierarchy of information, etc, etc.) get considered in their turn, each having an influence on how the design is developed, as the process of synthesis gathers pace.

At the end of it all is a pack, or perhaps a range of packs. A ridiculous amount of thought and effort goes into it. But then this is the very embodiment of your brand's values we're talking about, the thing that can make or break its sale, and the tangible bond in its relationship with your consumers.

SUMMARY

The purpose of design planning:

1. To define the correct proposition and personality for your brand.

2. To identify and express the one key thought that lies at the heart of the brief.

3. To help understand and strike the right balance between buyers and users.

4. To study the store environment and customers to understand how the brand works at point-of-sale.

5. To get to know the whole brand family and understand its relations.

6. To resolve the hierarchy of information relevant to your brand through determining the communication tasks and understanding the consumer's 'decision tree'.

7. To isolate category equities from brand equities.

8. Ultimately to create the best possible creative brief for the designers.

The designer's job:

9. To have the big idea.

10. To fit it with the best execution.

11. To synthesize the executional considerations and balance all aspects of the creative brief to create the Totally Branded pack.

8

HOW TO JUDGE IT

ASSESSING CREATIVE WORK

At several points during the course of a packaging design project, creative work will be formally presented for your approval. Even if your design consultancy believes in a truly interactive approach, and has involved you along the way in interim meetings, 'tissue' meetings and the like, there will still be a handful of occasions (the concept recommendation, the culmination of the design development phase, the first highly finished 3D mock-up) when, with varying degrees of theatricality, the work up to that point will be put before you and your response awaited.

What do you do? What do you say? There they sit, the whole design consultancy team, breath collectively bated, waiting for your word. They've been working really hard on it, they obviously think they've cracked it, and they now need your approval before they can move on to the next stage.

You are now suffering from horribly conflicting emotional pressures. On the one hand, there is the almost overwhelming pressure, emanating from the design team, of their desire for a positive response.

On the other hand, there is the pressure of your own equally strong desire to point out what is wrong with what has just been presented to you, and suggest an improvement. It's human nature. The first instinct of all of us, on being presented with a piece of creative work of any kind, is to find fault with it.

And fault there is bound to be, because you have either been presented with something totally uncontroversial, something which is so conventional, that you almost feel you've seen it before (in which case the fault is it's dull, boring and so lacking in originality that you might as well have done it yourself), or else you have been presented with something which contains at least a modicum of originality (in which case there is bound to be a 'fault' because at least one 'rule' will have been broken).

Fortunately, you know all this. So you know that immediately finding fault is not the appropriate response. So what is? Well, first of all, you have to consider exactly what it is that you are being asked to assess here. This might seem obvious, but it's actually surprisingly easy to make the wrong assumption on this score, and end up having a confusing discussion in which you and the design consultancy are talking at cross-purposes the whole time.

You are not necessarily being asked to approve the whole thing each time your design firm puts something visual in front of you. Think where you are up to in the process. At different stages, different aspects of the overall brief come to the fore, and you should be concentrating primarily on those. Of course, it's largely the responsibility of your design consultancy, in the way in which they present and talk about their work at each stage, to establish those criteria for you, and to help you to focus on the right thing. But it helps if you know what you are supposed to be looking at anyway.

In general, then, the principal 'milestone' creative presentations during the course of a project, and the key criteria against which you should be assessing the work in each case, are as follows:

Concept Recommendation

There may or may not have been an interim meeting or two leading up to this, in which a range of initial ideas may have been discussed. If so, what you are now being presented with should not be a total surprise. If not, what you are now looking at may seem to have arrived from Mars (I mean the planet, not the confectionery firm).

In either case, what you should be concentrating on at this point is the concept – the idea. You have only two important questions to ask yourself: (a) 'Is there an idea here?' and if so, (b) 'Does it communicate the agreed brand proposition?'

Now this is where the confusion often arises. In order to present the idea at all, your design consultancy will probably have drawn it up as a pack. So there are points of execution to look at as well, which may be helping or obscuring your appreciation of the idea, and which are bound in any case to raise a whole bunch of issues of their own.

Try to put questions of execution, for the moment at least, to one side. Focus purely on the idea. (Sometimes your design consultancy will have been brave enough and/or imaginative enough to find a way of presenting the idea *without* at this stage executing it as a pack, in which case you job will be easier. When we first presented the new Tango design idea to Britvic, we simply put on the table an orange with a ring-pull stuck in the top of it; there was no execution to respond to, only the idea in its purest form.)

If the idea itself is wrong, then there's no point in discussing anything else. Tell them why you think the idea misses the mark, and send them away to come up with another one.

I'm being very black and white here, of course, and in truth there are circumstances (alcoholic drinks brands, for example) in which ideas need to be extremely subtle, and are very difficult to divorce from execution. Nevertheless, in the vast majority of cases, ideas and executions *can* be separated – and for purposes of assessing creative recommendations at this stage, they should be.

So what if the idea is strong, and seems to communicate the brand's proposition (or at least to have the potential to do so if properly executed)?

First, tell them so. They now know that they haven't been wasting their time. You are on board with their most important creative output up to this point – the core idea.

Now, if there are executional issues to talk about, fine. They will almost certainly not have resolved the final execution in their own minds yet anyway, so will be only too happy to solicit your input at this stage.

DESIGN DEVELOPMENT PRESENTATION

This may come before or after qualitative research to solicit the consumer's input. Often there will be two such presentations – one prior to research, another later, after taking any research findings on board.

Whichever is the case, the focus has now shifted towards executional issues. The core idea should now be taken as read (though it's worth periodically checking that the idea is still shining though, and hasn't been obscured or even destroyed by the process of executional development which has taken place since you approved it).

The key criterion to consider now is brand personality. Overall, is the execution of this pack, or range of packs, such that the right brand personality is being conveyed? If so, great – we can now move on to talk about comparatively easy stuff. If not, hold it right there, because something fundamental has gone wrong.

Either way, the important thing is to keep referring back to the brief, to the agreed set of brand personality attributes. You shouldn't need to discuss design elements as such (colour, type, layout, etc), and indeed it is dangerous to do so, as it leads to you giving directional guidance of the wrong kind. It is perfectly legitimate, though, to say (for example): 'I thought we'd agreed this brand should be feminine and elegant; I'm afraid it all looks rather too masculine to me at the moment.' Let *them* worry about which particular elements or design features (assuming they accept your point) are contributing to that feeling of masculinity – that's what you're paying them for. They may be able to fix the problem in ways that you wouldn't have thought of.

Having dealt with brand personality, you can now move on to discuss other executional issues:

- *Brand equities.* If you're dealing with an existing brand, and if key equities were shown to exist during the planning phase, have these equities been respected, either by retaining them, building on them, or changing them to capture more strongly the worth that they held in the first place?

- *Category equities.* Is it as clear as it needs to be which category or frame of reference this brand belongs to?

■ *Variant differentiation.* Clear enough, or not?

■ *Brand family structure.* Where relevant, are the relationships between different members of a brand family sufficiently clear, and handled in the right ways?

■ *Hierarchy of information.* Thinking from a consumer's perspective, do you get everything out of the design that you need to get, in the right order of priority?

■ *Competitive context.* Is each pack differentiated to an appropriate degree, and in the right way, from its immediate competitors?

And so on, through any other issues that the brief required should be addressed.

It should be possible to give detailed and useful feedback to your design consultancy without ever once passing comment on particular design features or elements – only on whether or not it meets the brief in all respects. (It should even be possible, if you're some kind of saint, to keep your subjective likes and dislikes out of it. But we'll come on to those in a moment.)

One final word of caution here: it is impossible for a piece of packaging design work to fulfil every aspect of a brief with equal perfection. Somewhere along the way, a trade-off or two will have to be made, accepting 'good enough' on one dimension in order to achieve 'great' on another. But if your hardest task at this point is to judge whether the right trade-offs are being made, then you have relatively little to worry about: this project is going the right way.

Final Artwork Presentation

On those rare occasions when the creative solution is purely typographic, your task at this point is a simple check for accuracy.

More often, though, you will now be looking at final photography, or illustrations, or calligraphy as well.

If so, the key point to make here is that you should not be looking for a literal translation of the designer's rough visuals you have seen at earlier stages. It should now be much better.

This can be difficult to judge, because you are now used to the roughs, and probably had a good idea in your own mind's eye of what the finished result was going to look like.

151

So how do you judge if what you are now looking at is 'better'? Again, back to the brief!

WHAT TO DO IF YOU HATE THE WORK

With the best will in the world, you are only human, it's *your* brand, and you can't help but have subjective opinions about creative work presented to you.

This is fine so long as those subjective opinions coincide with the designers'. But what if they don't? What if you hate what they have put in front of you? It's technically 'on brief' but you hate it.

This brief section is to recommend three steps you should take before rejecting it out of hand.

Give it Time

You would not be the first person to hate a piece of work on sight, because it's not what you were expecting, only to come to love it once you gave it a chance to grow on you. So give it some time – at least the proverbial 'overnight test', and ideally longer.

Involve Others Close to the Brand

By this I do *not* mean the 'quick-and-dirty-bit-of-research-around-the-office' which involves soliciting an instant like/dislike reaction from half a dozen secretaries and a couple of passing sales managers (a research methodology whose findings invariably turn out to be directly opposite to the findings of the more conventional kind of research involving your actual consumers). What I mean is, seek the opinions of other members of the broader brand team discussed in Chapter 5: your ad agency people, your PR agency, your trade marketing team.

They, with a knowledge of the brand and with its interests at heart, but with perhaps less clearly formed expectations than your own, might well be able to persuade you of merits in the work which had at first passed you by.

Then again (and especially if they know that you hate it) they might hate it too. In which case ...

Consider Deferring to the Consumer

Here I'm on dangerous ground. For all the virtues of consumer research, I would not normally argue for its use as a substitute for judgement, rather as an aid to it.

But these are special circumstances. You passionately believe this creative work to be wrong, yet your design consultancy appears to believe equally passionately that it's right.

I think in these circumstances, unless you've hired a really duff design consultancy, you have to accept the possibility that they might be right. You might simply be a poor judge of design (no shame in that – some of our top captains of industry wouldn't know a good piece of packaging design if it made their early morning tea for them).

So if your design consultancy sticks firmly to its guns, let the work progress at least to qualitative research. Then, if the consumer sees no merit in it either, fire them (the designers, not your consumers!).

RESEARCHING THE CONCEPT: HOW NOT TO DO IT

There is a depressingly frequent abuse of qualitative consumer research which involves putting in a whole raft of different design concepts and asking the consumer to 'pick a winner'.

This is the wrong way to do it, for several reasons.

Qualitative Research is for Understanding, not Evaluation

Picking a winner from several options is an essentially evaluative task. As such, for the results to be reliable, it needs a representative and robust sample of the brand's target market. In other words, it needs a quantitative research methodology.

Qualitative research (depth interviews or, more commonly, group discussions) on the other hand is simply not designed for such tasks. The numbers involved are too small to be relied upon, and the unstructured nature of the discussions means that findings cannot reliably be compared from one group to the next.

153

The whole point of qualitative research is to go beneath the surface of consumer opinions and behaviour, to arrive at a deeper understanding of *why* they think as they do, or *why* they behave in a particular way.

As such, qualitative research is particularly useful as a design development tool, but only if properly used. We'll come on to discuss the right way to use it shortly. For the moment, suffice it to say that an important consideration in using it properly is that the research should not be overloaded with too much material, but should focus on getting more out of less.

Strategy and Design Become Confused

Often, the reason several designs are put into this kind of research is because several alternative design *strategies* are still under consideration (perhaps alternative propositions, or alternative brand personalities) and different designs have been created to represent each strategic option.

This, in my experience, is extremely dangerous. Consumers will, understandably, respond to what they see in front of them. Unless each strategic option has been 'represented' by an equally strong design, there is a real danger of the 'wrong' one winning. Let's suppose that one of the strategic routes is inherently better than the others – more distinctive, more motivating, more exciting in its potential to build the brand – but let's suppose that there is an executional flaw or two in the design that has been created to 'represent' that route (the colours are all wrong, let's say, or the type's not quite right). Now let's suppose that there is another, inherently weaker, strategy, but one which is being 'represented' by a design which in executional terms presses more of the right buttons.

With the best research moderator in the world, the latter of those two options will 'win'. Yet the executional failings of the first, and stronger, route might easily have been ironed out in subsequent development, to produce a much better 'winner'. Only now it will never happen because that route will be abandoned.

For research purposes, strategy and design should be kept apart. If there are strategic options to be explored, they should be researched back in the design planning phase, before the creative brief is written and certainly before any serious design work is done. And in terms of stimulus materials, anything but pack designs should be used – word sorts, image boards, narrative tapes, you name it. Anything but packs.

By the time we get to design development research, therefore, the strategy should already have been decided upon. What we are researching now is how well (or not) a proposed design is capable of delivering against that strategy.

The Safest (and therefore least safe) Design will Win

Even if all the designs have been created to the same strategy, there is another reason for resisting the temptation to put multiple options into this kind of research.

Experience shows that consumers will, in these circumstances, tend to prefer the most obviously 'safe' design – the one which fits most happily with their expectations. This is because, in the research situation, all the candidate designs are denied the credibility and authenticity that would instantly accrue to them were they encountered in the real shopping environment in real life.

Lacking such reassurance about any of them, consumers will usually be drawn to the design which seems the most credible and authentic – the 'safest' one, in other words, the one that looks most like such things normally look. But is this really the safest design to proceed with, in terms of its likelihood of building the brand? Almost certainly not.

RESEARCHING THE CONCEPT: A BETTER WAY

The ideal use of qualitative research as a design development tool is to focus on a single proposed concept. If (as will often be the case) more than one concept has been created and presented to the client, the collective judgement of the team should be used to select the one to go into research.

This is not so wildly gung-ho a view as it might appear. After all, if the right work has been done at the design planning stage (which may very well have included consumer research to explore strategic options, and/or to investigate category and brand equities) then the creative brief should be pretty watertight.

155

So we know, among other things, what proposition we are trying to communicate, and what brand personality to convey. These being the fundamentals of Total Branding, the main differences in any different concepts presented thus far will be either (a) different *ideas* to communicate the proposition, and/or (b) different *executions* of an idea to convey the right brand personality.

On most projects in my experience, assessing which is the strongest candidate idea, and which execution of it comes closest to capturing the desired brand personality, is not too difficult given the collective experience and judgement of the team. And it's not for this that consumer research is really needed.

Rather, the role of research at this stage is to provide consumer input and guidance to help optimize the final design as it goes through the processes of development and refinement. It's about improving rather than choosing; perfecting rather than selecting.

For qualitative research to be used in this way immediately avoids all the pitfalls identified in the previous section, and plays to its true strengths as a diagnostic, as opposed to an evaluative, tool.

With just the one concept to explore (or at most, a couple of variations on the same concept) time can be devoted to an in-depth understanding of its strengths and weaknesses against the agreed strategy.

Ideally, it should be exposed to consumers in the form of highly finished 3D mock-ups, presented without comment as part of a competitive set. Here we can get our first key piece of learning: how readily is it accepted by consumers? If it's a redesign of an existing brand, does it elicit comments such as 'Oh, I haven't seen that *x* pack before; my shop must still be stocking the old ones' (at which point, any fears that the proposed concept might be too radical can be dismissed) or is it treated with suspicion, giving rise to comments such as 'That's not *x*. I wonder what it is?' (in which case, maybe it *is* too radical, depending on what is subsequently said about it).

More detailed exploration should *not* be via direct questioning regarding elements of the design (they'll honestly try to help, but design works at far too subconscious a level for consumers usefully to articulate what they think of a particular typeface or a particular colour combination) but rather via indirect questions using projective techniques to explore in detail what the proposed design is or is not communicating.

What sort of people would use this brand? What (unless the product itself is already very familiar to them) would you expect the product to be like? What's the company like that makes this?

More ambitiously, and handled by a skilled moderator: What sort of person would this brand be if it literally came to life? What political party would it vote for? What newspapers does it read?

One of my favourite techniques, for the richness of learning it provides, is to hand out cartoons showing a rough sketch of the proposed new design (this, obviously, after the group has been exposed to it for a while) sitting next to its principal competitor, each with a thought-bubble above it, in which consumers are asked to fill in what each is thinking about the other.

The findings from this sort of research can be enormously helpful in guiding final development. And once these fundamental brand communication issues have been dealt with, there will still be time to explore the more straightforward issues of variant differentiation, hierarchy of information, etc.

Very occasionally, qualitative research done in this way will result in the conclusion that the proposed concept is fundamentally flawed and should be abandoned (at which point everyone wishes more concepts had been put into the research!). But when this happens, it is invariably because of some fundamental error back at the design planning stage (like the wrong strategy being adopted!). And there's no guarantee that this concept – which we now know to be fundamentally flawed – would not have actually emerged unscathed from the more superficial analysis to which it would have been subjected had it gone alongside half a dozen others into a 'pick-a-winner' exercise. It might even have won!

So, for my two penn'orth, the risk of being set back several weeks by abandoning the 'safety in numbers' approach in favour of 'perfecting our best', only to find it all going horribly wrong, is overwhelming outweighed by the benefits of enhanced understanding and more detailed development guidance which using research in this way yields.

FINAL EVALUATION PRE-LAUNCH

Increasingly these days, and particularly if qualitative research has been used during the design development process, new packs are launched onto the market without any final quantitative evaluation.

Sometimes the project has built up such a head of steam by now, and so many people are committed to its success, that the prospect of falling at the final hurdle, and having all that work wasted, is just too awful to contemplate.

There are *good* reasons, too, for not conducting a final quantitative test, not the least of them being that markets are changing ever faster, and time is these days a significant competitive weapon. Quantitative research adds another month or two to the timetable, and sometimes the risk of delaying the launch or relaunch is judged to be greater than the risk, by now, of getting it wrong.

This can be particularly true in the case of NPD projects, where in any case the packaging is only one of a whole mix full of interlinked variables, and may be pointless by now to research in isolation.

But there are still many instances, especially when a major brand is being relaunched in new packaging, when it will be prudent to conduct a final quantitative evaluation of the new against the old packaging.

Such research is fraught with difficulties, however, so there are some important points that need to be borne in mind.

Make it as Real as Possible

By now, you are looking for accurate predictions of marketplace performance. So the closer you can get to replicating marketplace conditions, the better. Research using mock-ups in the real shopping environment if at all possible. If not, and you have to use hall-tests, get mocked-up fixtures into the halls if you can.

At the very least, use 3D pack mock-ups rather than

photographs or slides. The world is full of packs which look better, and communicate quicker, in real life than they do in photographs. And vice versa. If you have to use photos or slides, you might as well not bother, because the results will be too far removed from reality to be of any use.

For the same reason, avoid the dreaded T-scope like the plague. The pseudo-scientific analysis of recognition speeds and eye-movements which T-scopes offer are obtained in a way so alien to how people actually browse whilst shopping that the whole exercise would be comical if it weren't so expensive.

Use Matched Monadic Samples

In other words, don't take one sample of consumers and ask them to compare old and new designs against one another. The findings will be massively distorted by the 'familiarity effect' which will work either for or against the old design (and to make matters worse, you won't know which).

Instead, recruit two samples of consumers (matched on all dimensions – age, sex, brand usage, etc – which are likely to be influential) and research the old pack against the competition with one sample, the new pack against the competition with the other. Then compare the results between the two.

Test Communication, Not Liking

It doesn't necessarily matter whether the consumers 'like' your pack. In some markets it does, in others not. What's more important is that the pack communicates the right things about the brand. So make sure the research agency constructs a tailored questionnaire based on your brand's design strategy, and doesn't just use an off-the-shelf, all-purpose pack design questionnaire.

Ask About the Brand First, then About the Pack

Even with matched monadic samples, the 'familiarity effect' can get in the way. The sample exposed to the new pack will probably spot straight away that it is the pack design that is being researched, so they will answer as design critics. But the sample exposed to the old pack, even if the questions are phrased so as to focus their attention on the design, will tend to answer in terms of what they feel about the brand rather than about its pack. For them, the pack has become a symbol of the brand (as the new one will, given half a chance, but it doesn't enjoy that status yet).

There's no perfect solution to this problem that I'm aware of, but making a point of first asking questions about the brand *per se*, and only then about the pack design, may go some way towards minimizing this effect.

Ultimately, although quantitative evaluations are difficult, a new design should win hands down if it is good enough.

And if it has been created to deliver Total Branding, it should be.

SUMMARY

1. Refer to the brief to assess and make constructive criticisms at each stage – concept recommendation, design development presentation, final artwork presentation.

2. Three steps to take if you hate the work: give it time; involve others with knowledge of the brand; use qualitative research to assess the design with consumers.

3. How *not* to research – don't use the 'pick-a-winner' approach but use the right type of research for the task in hand; keep strategy and design separate.

4. How to research – select a single concept to research; use research to improve rather than choose, perfect rather than select; use indirect questions and projective techniques to find out what the proposed design is communicating.

5. Where quantitative research is used as a final evaluation pre-launch: make it real; avoid T-scopes; use matched monadic samples; focus on communication, not likes and dislikes; beware the 'familiarity effect'.

BIBLIOGRAPHY

Behaeghel, J (1991) *Brand Packaging, The Permanent Medium*, Architecture & Design Technology Press.

Berger, J (1972) *Ways of Seeing*, BBC & Penguin Books.

Doyle, P 'UK Marketing Guide: The Importance of Brand Building', *Marketing*, 6 July 1989.

Doyle, P 'Rules for Global Brands', *Campaign*, 15 June 1990.

Doyle, P Interview with *Marketing*, 9 March 1989.

Eco, U (1979) *A Theory of Semiotics*, Macmillan.

Feldwick, P (1991) 'Defining a Brand', *Understanding Brands*, Kogan Page.

Femina, D and Sopkin (1970) From: *Those Wonderful Folk who gave you Pearl Harbour*, Pitman Publishing.

Interbrand–Mercury Business Books (1990) *Brands – An International Review*, Golden Arrow Publications.

Jung, C (1978) *Man and his Symbols*, Picador Publication, Pan Books.

Kapferer, J-N (1992) *Strategic Brand Management*, Kogan Page.

James, W (1958) *The Varieties of Religious Experience*, Modern Library, New York.

King, S 'Tomorrow's Research – Brand Building, Pressures on Marketing and the Implications for Future Market Research Methods', *Admap*, September 1991.

King, S Interview with *Marketing*, 16 March 1989.

King, S (1991) 'Brand Building in the 1990's, *Journal of Marketing Management*, pp 7, 1, 3–13.

Lewis, M (1991) 'Brand Packaging', *Understanding Brands*, Kogan Page.

Maslow, A H (1978) *Motivation and Personality*, 3rd ed, Harper & Row, New York.

Minale, M (1991) *How to Run a Successful Multi-Disciplinary Design Company*, Elfande.

Ogilvy, D (1993) *Ogilvy on Advertising*, Pan Books Ltd.

Olins, W (1989) *Corporate Identity*, Thames & Hudson.

O'Malley, D (1987) 'Creative Briefing', *How to Plan Advertising*, Cassell in association with the Account Planning Group.

Packard, V (1958) *The Hidden Persuaders*, Pocket Books Inc.

163

Peters, M 'Logomania' *Campaign*, 6 December 1991.

Pilditch, J (1972) *The Silent Salesman*, 2nd ed, Business Books.

Ries, A and Trout, J (1986) *Positioning, the Battle for Your Mind*, McGraw Hill Book Company.

Wickens, M 'War Dance', *Creative Review*, April 1993.

Woodward, S (1991) 'Competitive Marketing', *Understanding Brands*, Kogan Page.

REFERENCES

1. Page 18, quote by Peter Doyle – 'UK Marketing Guide: The Importance of Brand Building', *Marketing*, 6 July 1989.
2. Page 77, studies by Peter Doyle – 'UK Marketing Guide: The Importance of Brand Building', *Marketing*, 6 July 1989.
3. Ibid.

INDEX

Rosser Reeves, USP (Unique Selling Proposition) 51

Sainsbury, own-label goods 25–6
saliency of brand equities 61–3, 64, 132
Sanatogen, synergy between advertising and packaging 76
self-service shopping *see* supermarkets
shelf impact, and brand share 102
Silhouette, synergy between advertising and packaging 76
Skol lager, packaging and brand repositioning 34
SMART principle, and marketing objectives 101
SmithKline Beecham, brand repositioning of Lucozade 34–5
Soft & Gentle deodorant, relaunch of 39–40
Sol (Mexican beer), iconic significance 32
Southern Comfort, active equities on logo 62
strategic discipline and Total Branding 67–8, 79
style, role in packaging design 53–4
supermarkets
and categorized perception 57–8
influence on packaging design 22–3
point of sale observation 124–7, 143

SWOT analysis of brands 101

Tango fruit drink 72, 90–1
core idea of packaging design 51–2
ring pull fruit idea 74, 149
style of design 53–4
target markets
defining in client briefs 103–4
defining as individuals 103
technical developments, DAR (Digital Artwork Reproduction) 88–9
Terry's of York, Pyramint 52
Tesco
own-label goods 25–6
Value range 25
Tetley tea 74
Tetrapak, structural innovations 39
Tetrapaks, for drinks 57
texture 75
influence in Total Branding 45
and packaging design 40–1
Tide, packaging design 21
time limits in client briefs 106
Toilet Duck, design of pack shape 38, 72
Tomy 'Big Fun' toys 52–3, 72, 74
observation at point of sale 126–7
Total Branding
as barrier to competition 71–2
basis in brand strategy 121
and brand extension 72–4, 79